America's
Great Gun Game

America's Great Gun Game

Gun Ownership vs. Americans' Safety

An Outline of the Need for Increased Federal Gun Legislation

EARL E. MCDOWELL
Author of *Interviewing Practices for Technical Writers and Research in Scientific and Technical Communication*

iUniverse, Inc.
New York Lincoln Shanghai

America's Great Gun Game
Gun Ownership vs. Americans' Safety

iUniverse books may be ordered through booksellers or by contacting:

iUniverse
2021 Pine Lake Road, Suite 100
Lincoln, NE 68512
www.iuniverse.com
1-800-Authors (1-800-288-4677)

Because of the dynamic nature of the Internet, any Web addresses or links contained in this book may have changed since publication and may no longer be valid.

The views expressed in this work are solely those of the author and do not necessarily reflect the views of the publisher, and the publisher hereby disclaims any responsibility for them.

ISBN: 978-0-595-43032-1 (pbk)
ISBN: 978-0-595-87373-9 (ebk)

Printed in the United States of America

Contents

Preface

Did you know that firearms kill over thirty thousand Americans every year? Did you know that firearms killed more than 1.5 million Americans during the twentieth century? Throughout the twentieth century, gun control advocates and gun rights supporters were involved in a series of "gun games." In most cases, the gun rights groups—most significantly the NRA—won these games.

This book contains ten chapters:

Chapter 1: The Beginning of America's Great Gun Game

Chapter 2: The Second Amendment and the National Rifle Association

Chapter 3: Assassinations and Attempted Assassinations of Presidents, an Ex-President, and Presidential Candidates

Chapter 4: Gun Movements from 1922 through 1968

Chapter 5: Gun Movements from 1986 to Today

Chapter 6: Guns and Women

Chapter 7: Guns and Children

Chapter 8: Handguns

Chapter 9: Concealed Handguns

Chapter 10: Reality Time

This book was written for the general public. As you begin to read this book, I ask you to be an active reader. Initially, please take the Pretest Gun Game Questionnaire. You can then go to the Meaning of Test Results section of the book to determine whether you support a pro-gun control side, a pro-gun side or if you are undecided. Several pencil-and-paper questionnaires are given throughout the book. These should help you refine your thinking on the gun issue. Are you ready to play the gun game?

Pretest
Gun Game Questionnaire

Please answer the following questions. Write "yes" in the space provided if you agree with the statement. Write "no" if you disagree with the statement.

1. _____ The Second Amendment of the Constitution guarantees all law-abiding citizens the "right to bear arms."

2. _____ The NRA is concerned about the welfare of children.

3. _____ There should be a national registration of all handguns.

4. _____ Gun makers should be held legally responsible for selling guns to illegal gun dealers.

5. _____ The federal government should require serial numbers on all firearms.

6. _____ When a person purchases a gun, he/she should be photographed.

7. _____ There should be a national licensing of all handgun owners.

8. _____ A ban on any firearm is a ban on all firearms.

9. _____ Buy back programs, although well intentioned, are a waste of time and money.

10. _____ Citizens who carry concealed weapons do not commit crimes with those weapons.

11. _____ A law-abiding citizen should be permitted to carry a concealed weapon to church.

12. _____ Handgun ownership by the general public should be banned.

13. _____ More concealed weapons equals less crime.

14. _____ The government should allow ammunition shipments through the U.S. Postal Service.

15. _____ Self-defense with a gun is a God-given right.

16. _____ Our country will be safest when all law-abiding citizens have guns to ensure their safety.

17. _____ I would like a "pocket rocket."

18. _____ All gun owners should be licensed.

19. _____ The federal government should ban the mail-order sale of firearms.

20. _____ Guns don't kill people; people kill people.

Now that you have completed the pretest, go to the end of the book and read the "Meaning of the Test Results" section.

1

The Beginning of America's Great Gun Game

Would to God that this unhappy weapon had never been devised ... and that so many brave and valiant men had never died by the hands of those ... who would not dare to look in the face of those whom they lay low with their wretched bullets. They are tools invented by the devil to make it easier to kill each other.[1]

—Blaise de Montluc

Can we stop the cancer (proliferation of guns) from spreading, or is the gun crisis terminal?

How can gun control advocates win the gun game?

I grew up in Dora, Pennsylvania, a rural coal mining community near Punxsutawney, home of the famous groundhog. I began hunting when I was twelve although I remember shooting marks at a much earlier age. I enjoyed hunting and shooting throughout my teenage years. We had six guns in our house, including my grandfather's single-shot .32-20 rifle.

I have memories of several childhood incidents involving guns. I often played cops and robbers at my neighbor's house. My friend would chase his brother and me around the house while pointing a real pistol at us. We were scared at times, but I have no idea whether or not the gun was loaded. In the 1950s, it was quite common for boys in our community to carry BB guns or .22s. We didn't think about shooting another person, but we enjoyed shooting at tin cans, birds and groundhogs. Once, one of my friends shot his brother in the buttocks with a BB gun. We all laughed, except for the boy who had been shot.

I lived about a mile from the Dora post office, and every day except Sunday I usually ran there to pick up the mail. Sometimes I would walk through the woods, and sometimes I would run down Dora hill. When I walked through the woods, I would carry my BB gun or .22. When I ran on the highway, I would carry rocks for protection, which I also enjoyed throwing at fence posts.

One summer day in 1954, when I was twelve years old, I was running down Dora hill when a man in a pickup truck stopped and asked if I wanted a ride. "No, thank you," I said. I saw a shotgun leaning against the truck's passenger seat, but I was quite naive and didn't even consider that I might be in danger. After I refused the ride, he exposed himself and said that he wanted me to touch his private area. I responded quickly by throwing the rocks I was carrying at him, and I ran down the hill. I was approximately a half-mile from the Dobson store in Dora. As I ran under the railroad bridge about a hundred yards from the store, I looked back. The man had turned his truck around and was chasing me. When he saw me run under the bridge, he turned around and drove back up the hill. I ran to a neighbor's house and told him the story. He drove me home. I often wonder what I would have done if I had been carrying my BB gun or .22. Would I have shot the man in the truck?

After graduating from Punxsutawney Senior High School in 1961, I enrolled at Clarion State College, where I majored in speech communication and minored in history. On November 22, 1963, President John F. Kennedy was assassinated. At the time, I didn't think about how the assassin had obtained the gun he had used to kill the president.

It was during this time that I learned about the Second Amendment. In two of my speech classes, I gave presentations supporting it. I also debated the issue in classes and for the debate team. If you know anything about formal debate, you know that a debater must be prepared to argue both for (pro) and against (con) a given position. Debating provided an excellent academic experience, but in my real world, I still supported gun rights. During this period, I also became aware of the National Rifle Association (NRA) and its publications. *American Rifleman* became my Bible when debating against gun control and for the Second Amendment. I often think about this time and how naive I was not to question the NRA's facts about our Founding Fathers, the Second Amendment, and the statistics used to support its viewpoint.

Near the end of my undergraduate studies in 1965, a friend who owed me eight dollars gave me a nonfunctional pistol as payment. I kept the gun under the driver's seat in my car for protection. After graduating from college, I accepted a position as a speech and English teacher and the director of dramatics at the Utica Free Academy in Utica, New York. For almost three years, the pistol under the driver's seat gave me a sense of security, especially when I was driving back and forth between Punxsutawney and Utica. I never really thought of pointing the gun at anyone until April 4, 1968—the day Dr. Martin Luther King Jr. was assassinated. On that day, I had been holding a dress rehearsal for a play I was directing at the academy. It was quite common for me to drive students home after rehearsal. Many of my students were black, and I gave some of them a lift that day, unaware that Dr. King had been killed. As I was driving back to my apartment, traffic suddenly came to a standstill. My car was quickly surrounded by African Americans, who began to rock it back and forth. I was incredibly frightened. I remembered the nonfunctional pistol under my seat, but I really didn't know what to do. Should I sit quietly and wait for the police to disperse the crowd? Should I take the pistol from under the seat and point it at the people who were rocking my car? Should I try to get out of my car and run? Fortunately, I had the common sense to remain stationary. I waited for about thirty minutes, until the crowd was dispersed by the police. I often think about what would have happened to me if I had pointed the nonfunctional gun at the crowd. I often wonder what I would have done if the gun had been functional and loaded.

After teaching for three years at the Utica Free Academy, I returned to Pennsylvania, where I taught junior high English for Kiski Public Schools near Vandergrift, Pennsylvania. I also taught speech fundamentals two nights a week at Pennsylvania State University in New Kingston, Pennsylvania. My nonfunctional pistol remained under my seat, and I felt secure.

In 1970, I enrolled in the master's program in speech communication at West Virginia University. During the fall semester, I started to think about a possible topic for my master's thesis. After reading several articles on gun rights in *American Rifleman*, I decided to focus my thesis on the gun issue. In fact, I was so excited about gun rights as a thesis topic that I only spent one week at home over the Christmas holidays before returning to Morgantown, West Virginia, to develop a proposal for my thesis. It was titled *A Study of the Rhetorical Events Leading to the Federal Gun Control Act of 1968.*[2]

During the beginning phase of my research, I limited my research to biased, pro-gun sources. Dr. Robert Perkowski, my adviser, was patient as he pointed out my biases and suggested that I use government documents and periodicals that presented different viewpoints. My thesis focused on gun control movements between 1922 and 1968. As I continued my research, I became more open-minded about gun control views. I was shocked by many references to the gun-saturated 1920s—how easy it was for anyone to purchase a handgun and, in most cases, the general lack of interest in Congress to pass federal and state gun legislation. Over a period of five months, I had switched from a pro-gun to a pro-gun-control viewpoint. This metamorphosis occurred as a result of reading thousands of pages of government documents and unbiased sources.

After finishing my master's degree, I enrolled in and completed a PhD program in speech communication at the University of Nebraska. I have been a professor at the University of Minnesota since 1973. Over the past thirty-three years, I have written two academic books and over one hundred academic articles. My interest in gun control, in terms of publishing, was put on the back burner. I do, however, continue to be an active reader on the subject and suggest that students in my public-speaking classes use the gun issue for their speeches of controversy or persuasion. I often provide students with the most recent sources to help them build a case supporting either a pro-gun or a pro-gun-control viewpoint.

I continued to read articles, editorials, and books on both sides of the issue but retained my pro-gun-control opinions. I was glued to C-SPAN and evening talk shows when the Violent Crime Control and Law Enforcement Act of 1994 and the Domestic Violence Offender Gun Ban Act of 1996 were discussed, debated, and passed.

It was not until 2000, however—after reading a column entitled "Don't Nullify Second Amendment Rights" in the *Punxsutawney Spirit*—that I became an active writer on the importance of gun control legislation.[3] I was offended by that column, as it claimed that the Million Mom March (MMM) took place for political reasons and that the marchers had been manipulated. I disagreed with this assertion. I had watched the march for several hours on C-SPAN, and it was clear to me that the participants had deep-seated and sincere feelings about the enforcement of present gun laws and safety measures. The march had provided women with an opportunity to express their viewpoints about gun violence against women and children. During the march, thousands of women had carried signs with pictures of wives, mothers, and children who had been killed by guns, while others carried signs that focused on gun registration and a common-sense approach to the gun problem.

In my response to the article, I indicated that I agreed with Donna Dees-Thomases—the primary organizer of the MMM—as well as many other speakers, including President Bill Clinton, Hillary Clinton, and Rosie O'Donnell, who asserted that the registration of guns (especially handguns) and the licensing of owners are necessary in order to make our society safer.

I also cited Homer Cummings, a former attorney general, and his appeal to the patriotism of all good Americans after the attempted assassination of Franklin D. Roosevelt. He indicated that no honest citizen could object to registration, a procedure much simpler than the registration and licensing procedure applicable to automobiles. "Show me a man," he said, "who doesn't want his gun registered, and I will show you a man who shouldn't have a gun."[4] I also cited Senator Robert Kennedy (D-NY), who said that "Regulation of the sale of firearms is, in my judgment, essential for the safety and welfare of the American people."[5]

I concluded my rebuttal by reporting the following statistics cited in *Newsweek*'s August 23, 1999 issue: 66 percent of gun owners support the idea of all handgun owners registering with the government; 45 percent support having hunting-rifle owners registering with the government; 80 percent support mandatory courses on gun safety, and almost all of them support having child safety locks on guns.[6]

In addition, I discussed the National Rifle Association (NRA). Wayne LaPierre, its executive vice president, had claimed that over twenty thousand gun laws weren't being enforced and that our country didn't need any more laws. If this had been true, I suggested, perhaps all of those already existing laws should have been reviewed, revised, and enforced so as to ensure a safer society. If new laws were needed, they should have been introduced and strictly enforced. I disagreed with LaPierre, suggesting that since thirty thousand citizens were killed each year by guns and four thousand of them were children, we needed comprehensive, reasoned solutions to the gun problem.[7]

Since publishing this editorial in the *Spirit*, I have continued to be an active reader and writer on the gun issue. My research indicates that over the past eighty years, many members of Congress have tried to pass federal gun legislation intended to decrease the number of murders, the number of suicides, and the number of accidental deaths in the United States. During the past thirty-five years, over one million citizens have been killed by firearms in the United States. The number of murders in the United States is nineteen times higher than the number of murders in thirty-five other high-income countries combined, and 77 percent of these homicides were committed with handguns.[8]

The NRA has been very successful in stopping significant federal and state gun legislation. It continues to fight against the licensing of gun owners and the registration of firearms. The NRA claims that law-abiding adult citizens have "the right to bear arms," which means that when formerly law-abiding citizens murder someone or commit a crime, they become lawless and should no longer be allowed to have a gun. The organization also supports the sale of mail-order rifles and assault weapons to law-abiding citizens. It also believes that parents should decide whether to have safety locks on their guns. This leads one to wonder whether NRA members believe that we should require car safety seats for children—perhaps, that also should be determined by parents alone? This is part of the NRA's gun game.

Even after the assassinations of President John F. Kennedy, Dr. Martin Luther King Jr., and Senator Robert Kennedy, the NRA continued to babble its slogans.

"Gun registration leads to gun confiscation."

"Guns don't kill people; people kill people."

Pressed on by these empty words, NRA members continue to write letters opposing any gun legislation to their members of Congress. These slogans are part of the NRA's gun game.

William Manchester, historian and author of *Death of a President*, responded to the repeated NRA statement that "Guns don't kill people; people kill people." First, however, he wrote about turning in his gun to the Hartford Connecticut Police Department. He claimed that his reason for surrendering the gun was one of conscience.

> But I rest better knowing that there is one American household from which the instrument of terror has been removed, one home where violence will remain a stranger, and one family which is free—to borrow a phrase from one who was a loving father—from the enemy within."[9]

The "enemy within," or temper, is inherent in each of us, and guns are frequently used when this enemy is stirred to anger. Here is his response to the NRA:

> Guns don't kill people, the NRA replied to the critics; people kill people. That was the cheap sophistry. People with guns kill people, and it is a sad comment on the mood of the nation since President Kennedy's murder that never in human history have so many people in the United States owned so many guns."[10]

In 2003, after reading several anti-gun-control editorials in the *Minnesota Daily*, the student newspaper at the University of Minnesota, I decided to respond to the ridiculous idea of allowing students and faculty members to carry concealed handguns to classes and sporting events. I submitted my editorial, "Ban Concealed Weapons at the U," to the *Daily*.[11] In this piece I discussed why concealed weapons should be banned at all University of Minnesota functions.

The *Daily* decided to make the editorial a web exclusive, and it was disseminated over the Internet. Within two days, I received over two hundred responses from all over the country, as well as from England, Canada, Germany, and Australia. Only thirty-one e-mails supported my viewpoint, and all but two supportive respondents were female. Here are four hateful responses:

> Why don't you go and masticate feces? You obviously didn't read the Second Amendment correctly when you penned your thesis. It's folks like you who make the appellation of America a disgrace.

> Thanks be to God you're not in control, Adolf, or we'd all lose our rights to peacefully carry. Hallelujah for the rights of Minnesota folks to carry!!! (Don't let that cause you to soil your baby-shaped Kimbies!)

> Real patriots don't try to deny the God-given RIGHT (Natural right, to heathens like you) of self-protection to ANYONE, especially their fellow citizens.

> How do people as ignorant as you ever get any sort of college degree?

> Please tell me where you received your diploma(s) as I would like to avoid that school.

Here, on the other hand, is one of the supportive responses:

> I am a student at the University and a big reader of the *Daily*. I read your editorial today (Monday, July 14) about concealed weapons and I just wanted to thank you for your article. As a student who is not only against the law, but also wanting to freely sit in class and attend football games without the threat of the person sitting next to me having a gun, I was very excited to read your piece. Having an expert opinion rather than someone who just likes to run their mouth on the subject was helpful. Thank you again for taking time to share your expertise on this issue with the University community. I hope that it affects others as much as it has affected me.

I have talked to over three hundred college students and more than thirty professors at the University of Minnesota, and none supports allowing students, faculty, or the general public to carry concealed weapons on campus. My experience, however, reinforces the idea that NRA members have deep-seated opinions about conceal-and-carry laws. They do not want registration of firearms and do not want to have to be licensed in order to carry them. They want to be allowed to carry concealed weapons on college campuses, including in classrooms and at sporting events. NRA members are prepared to play hardball with anyone who challenges their views regarding the Second Amendment. They truly believe that they have a "God-given right" to own as many firearms as they want and to do with them as they please.

After thirty-five years of researching the gun issue, I decided to write a book on the topic. I looked forward to the challenge. Gun advocates have called me many names, but I have tried to fight back with logic and common sense. The gun issue is not one of Democrats against Republicans, liberals against conservatives, or good against evil. It is an issue of life and death. I apologize to readers for having remained silent for so long—for having been part of the silent majority. I should have been sharing my expertise and viewpoints with the general public all along.

Over two hundred books, over one hundred thousand articles and editorials, and over one thousand government documents and pamphlets have been published on this topic. Thousands of sources are available on the Internet. The purpose of this book is not to replicate what others have written, but to assist you in becoming an active and critical reader on the gun issue. Whether we like it or not, we are all part of the gun game. Pro-gun and pro-gun-control groups are constantly trying to persuade the general public to become involved in the dialogue. Currently, the pro-gun lobby is winning the gun game. In the 1920s, there were approximately 20 million guns in the United States. Today, there are over 220 million guns. The NRA's membership has increased from three thousand five hundred in the 1920s to about four million today.

In this chapter, I have tried to establish my credibility on the gun issue. Chapter 2 challenges the NRA's interpretation of the Second Amendment. In Chapter 3, I trace the assassinations of four presidents and a presidential candidate, and I also describe the attempted assassinations of five presidents, a former president, and a presidential candidate. Most of them were shot or shot at with handguns. Chapters 4 and 5 present a detailed account of the gun movements from 1922 through 2002 and beyond. I conclude my description of each movement by determining whether gun-control advocates or gun-rights groups won that particular gun game.

The last five chapters focus on guns and women, guns and children, handguns, concealable weapons, and what I call "reality time." *America's Great Gun Game* is unique in that I report in Chapter 6 on women's organizations for gun control and organizations for gun rights. Similarly, I report in Chapter 7 on children's organizations for gun control and organizations for gun rights. Chapters 8 and 9 present statistical data on handguns and concealable weapons and ask the reader to assess what needs to be done to make our country safer. Finally, in

Chapter 10, I review the first nine chapters and appeal to the reader to become an active participant in gun-control organizations.

You have already begun to play the gun game by completing the questionnaire that appeared earlier in the book. Now, as you read the rest of the book, reflect on the questions posed by each chapter. At the end of the book, you will find the Meaning of Test Results section, where you can determine whether you strongly support, support, or slightly support gun control. You might even be undecided or against gun control.

As you read the book, please remain an active participant by completing the questionnaires that conclude each chapter except Chapter 3.

It is time to play the gun game, and the teams pit the active minority against the silent majority.

Key Quotation of Chapter 1

Regulation of the sale of firearms is, in my judgment, essential for the safety and welfare of the American people.

—Senator Robert Kennedy

2

The Second Amendment and the National Rifle Association

The very language of the Second Amendment refutes any argument that it was intended to guarantee every citizen an unfettered right to any type of weapon.[1]

—Former Supreme Court Chief Justice Warren Burger

The Second Amendment has been the subject of one of the greatest pieces of fraud. I repeat 'fraud,' on the American public by special interest groups that I have seen in my lifetime.[2]

—Former Supreme Court Chief Justice Warren Burger

A well-regulated Militia being necessary to the security of a free State, the right of the people to keep and bear Arms shall not be infringed.[3]

—U.S. Constitution. Second Amendment

Should the Second Amendment be revised to represent the needs of law-abiding citizens in the twenty-first century?

Does the NRA represent your viewpoint on the gun issue?

THE SECOND AMENDMENT

Since the Second Amendment's inception in 1791, its meaning has been discussed by constitutional scholars. Both pro-gun and pro-gun-control groups cite credible sources to support their viewpoints. The purpose of this chapter is not to review the federal and state cases that are cited in many books on the gun issue but to present the viewpoints of both sides. My intent is to help you to determine your own viewpoints on both the Second Amendment and the National Rifle Association. First, please think about the following questions:

- Does the Second Amendment guarantee all law-abiding citizens the right to bear arms?

- Does the Second Amendment only apply to a "well-regulated militia?"

- Is the National Guard the United States' "well-regulated militia?"

- What does the term "well-regulated" mean to you?

- Is the Second Amendment a collective right?

- Is the Second Amendment an individual right?

- Should the Second Amendment be revised for the twenty-first century?

- If so, how would you revise the amendment?

According to guncite.com, the original intent of the Second Amendment was to preserve and guarantee the pre-existing right of individuals to "keep and bear arms." It indicates that the militia clause was a declaration of purpose to preserve the people's right to "keep and bear arms" and was the method the framers chose to ensure the continuation of a "well-regulated militia." This pro-gun Web site also asserts that all law-abiding citizens have a right to use firearms for self-defense—but the language of the amendment doesn't suggest a constitutional right to keep and bear arms for hunting, target shooting, or self-protection.[4]

In contrast, Deborah Homsher concludes that the Second Amendment was "… composed more than two hundred years ago by men who lived in a different world—before repeating rifles, before the infected, intestinal rending of the civil war and the liberation of the nation's slaves, before the enfranchisement of women …" She goes on to say that "the right to keep and bear arms shall not be infringed" had not been intended to include servants, slaves, vagabonds, or females.[5]

James Brady, press secretary under President Ronald Reagan, reminds us that, at the time the Constitution was adopted, each state had its own militia. Noah Webster, in his 1828 dictionary, defined a militia as "able-bodied men organized into companies, regiments and brigades, with officers of all grades, and required by law to attend military exercises on certain days only, but at other times left to pursue their usual occupations."[6] Militias were limited to white males between the ages of eighteen and forty-five. Three times, the Supreme Court has concluded that the modern "well-regulated militia" is the National Guard, a state-organized military force of ordinary citizens serving as part-time soldiers, as was the case with early state militias. [7] The Supreme Court also ruled five times that the Constitution does not guarantee the free and clear right to own a gun.[8]

In 1986 Justice William Brennan stated that we need not read the Second Amendment exclusively

> through the eyes of a small group of white property-owning males who lived in a world utterly different than our own.... The ultimate question must be what do the words of the text mean in our time? For the genius of the Constitution rests not in any static meaning it might have had in the world that is dead and gone, but in the adaptability of its great principles to cope with current problems and current needs.[9]

R. William Ide, president of the American Bar Association, remarked on April 15, 1994, at a National Press Club event:

> It is time we overcome the destructive myth perpetuated by gun control opponents about the Second Amendment ... Federal and state courts have reached in this century a consensus interpretation of the Second Amendment that permits the exercise of broad power to limit private access of firearms by all levels of government ... It is time we get on with the business of treating guns with the respect they require and one small step toward that end is making it clear that regulating gun ownership does not violate the Constitution.[10]

Brady also doubted that

> the Founding Fathers imagined a time when over 30,000 people each year are dying from gun violence, when high powered military-style weapons like AK-47s with 30-round magazines are available on the streets, when a 14-year-old can take his father's gun and mow down his classmates, or when parents leave a loaded pistol around and a two year old can easily fire it.[11]

Today, approximately 70 percent of American citizens support reasonable gun-control laws as necessary to reduce the level of gun violence in the United States. It makes sense that the framers of the Constitution would agree. Finally, I agree with Constance Crooker, who reminds us that the Second Amendment says that a "well-regulated Militia" is necessary for the "security of a free State." Thus, it assumes that militia duty will be under state regulation, which mirrors the requirement of Article I, Section 8, Clause 16 of the Constitution. Today, however, most "militia" groups have no connection to a government body but are self-proclaimed, unorganized militias.[12]

Now, how do you feel about the Second Amendment?

Should the Second Amendment be updated to make it more applicable to the twenty-first century?

THE NATIONAL RIFLE ASSOCIATION

The National Rifle Association was founded in 1871 by Colonel William C. Church and General George Wingate, two Civil War veterans, in New York. Church indicated that its primary goal was to "... promote and encourage rifle shooting on a scientific basis."[13]

General Ambrose Burnside became the NRA's first president. In support of the NRA, the New York state legislature appropriated twenty-five thousand dollars to purchase a site on Long Island to be used as a rifle range. In 1880, when New York stopped subsidizing shooting matches, the NRA became inactive.

Twenty-three years later, in 1903, the NRA was revived. By 1906, the NRA was promoting youth programs, and in 1907 it moved its headquarters to Washington, D.C. In 1909, the NRA reinforced its ties with the military by amending its bylaws to allow five new board members to be appointed by the secretary of war, the secretary of the navy, and commanders of the National Guard. In 1912, Congress supported funding for shooting contests, and the National Defense Act of 1916 set aside three hundred thousand dollars for civilian marksmanship training. By the 1920s, the NRA's membership had grown to three thousand five hundred, and it was affiliated with over two thousand shooting clubs.[14]

Since its inception, the NRA has played a significant role in civilian firearm training. The organization claims that its 50,000 certified instructors train more than 750,000 gun owners a year. It also claims to have trained 1.5 million police officers, 17 million hunters, and millions of other people.[15]

Today, its youth programs remain the cornerstone of the NRA, with approximately one million young people participating in shooting-sports events sponsored by the NRA and its affiliate programs with 4-H, the Boy Scouts of America, the American Legion, the U.S. Jaycees, and others. On its Web site, the NRA paints itself as an organization that promotes "... firearm safety effort(s), firearm training, law-enforcement programs, junior shooting activities, women's issues, hunting services, recreational competitions, gun collecting, and defense of the Second Amendment."[16]

The NRA headquarters building has a sign that reads, "The right of people to bear arms shall not be infringed." Note that there is no reference here to the first part of the Second Amendment—"A well-regulated Militia being necessary to the security of a free State."[17] By not including the first part of the Second Amendment here, the NRA is ignoring that the Second Amendment is a collective right that refers to states establishing their own militias. The second amendment does not guarantee all law-abiding citizens the "right to bear arms."

The stated purposes and the objectives of the NRA are:

- To protect and defend the Constitution of the United States especially with reference to the inalienable rights of the individual American Citizen guaranteed by such Constitution to acquire, possess, transport, carry, transfer ownership of, and enjoy the right to use ...

- To promote public safety, law and order, and the national defense.

- To train members of law-enforcement agencies, the armed forces, the militia, and people of good repute in marksmanship and in the safe handling and efficient use of small arms.

- To foster and promote the shooting sports, including the advancement of amateur competitions in marksmanship at the local, state, regional, national, and international levels.

- To promote hunter safety and to promote and defend hunting as a shooting sport.[18]

NRA officials and members should be congratulated for their efforts to train men, women, and youth in using different types of firearms. Its officials and members, however, should be *castigated* for attempting to link these activities with the "right to bear arms."

Since its inception, the NRA has opposed all gun-control measures. In 1911, NRA President James Drain opposed New York's Sullivan laws with the now familiar claim that "such laws have the effect of arming the bad man and disarming the good one to the injury of the community."[19] In 1934, the NRA established its Legislative Affairs Division. *American Rifleman* published articles and editorials about the defense of the Second Amendment and asked members to become involved as advocates for the NRA's interpretation of the Second Amendment.

In 1975, the NRA formed its lobbying arm, the Institute for Legislative Action (ILA). The ILA publishes a newsletter called *Grassroots Activism* and has helped to defeat pro-gun-control legislators and legislation at the federal and state levels for the past thirty years. The newsletter exhorts members to "register to vote, monitor local media, participate in call-in radio and television programs, join the NRA-ILA's frontline volunteer program, mobilize your club, and spread the word."[20]

The NRA publishes *American Rifleman*, *The American Guardian*, and *American's First Freedom*. These magazines articulate the NRA's position on the Second Amendment. *American Rifleman* provides NRA members with timely information about federal and state gun-control measures and asks its members to support political candidates who support pro-gun viewpoints.[21]

The NRA opposes new gun-control legislation in favor of stricter enforcement of existing laws to prohibit convicted felons and violent criminals from possessing firearms and to increase sentences for gun-related crime. It also supports "right-to-carry" laws that expedite the process enabling law-abiding citizens in many states to carry concealed handguns. [22]

James Brady has concluded that the NRA's constitutional theory is a "calculated distortion of the text, history, and judicial interpretation of the Second Amendment."[23] Former U. S. Supreme Court Justice Warren Burger asserted that the NRA has perpetrated a "fraud on the American people."[24]

Former President George H. W. Bush relinquished his NRA membership in 1995, after having been outraged by a fundraising letter written by Wayne LaPierre, which had asserted that "If you have a badge, you have the government's go-ahead to harass, intimidate, and even murder law-abiding citizens."[25]

Former Harvard Law School Dean Erwin Griswold had this to say:

> ... to assert that the Constitution is a barrier to reasonable gun laws, in the face of unanimous judgment of the federal courts to the contrary, exceeds the limits of principled advocacy. It is time for the NRA and its followers in Congress to stop trying to twist the Second Amendment from a reasoned (if antiquated) empowerment for a militia into a bulletproof personal right for anyone to wield deadly weaponry beyond legislative control.[26]

Throughout this book, I shall discuss the NRA's role in opposing federal and state gun legislation. You will learn that the NRA continues to win gun games at both the federal and state levels. As you read, please reflect on the following questions:

How do you feel about the NRA?
Are you a member of the NRA?
If not, will you join the NRA?
Do you think that the NRA is interested in the welfare of the public?
Do you think that the NRA is primarily concerned about the gun industry?
Do you believe in the NRA's stated objectives?

YOUR VIEWPOINT

This chapter has focused on the Second Amendment and the NRA. Throughout the twentieth century, the meaning of the Second Amendment has been debated by constitutional scholars, lawmakers, the general public, and both gun-control and gun-rights groups.

The NRA has played a significant role in opposing gun-control measures. Throughout this book, I shall discuss its successes and failures, thereby aiding you in assessing the strategies and tactics the NRA has used to combat federal gun-control measures.

Now we are ready to examine the assassinations of and assassination attempts against presidents, an ex-president, and presidential candidates, as well as gun control movements, guns and women, guns and children, handguns, and conceal-and-carry laws. I shall also explain the need for all Americans to play an active role in the gun game.

As you read the following chapters, remember that the gun game is ongoing. At this point, do you support the gun-control side or the gun-rights side? Or are you undecided? Please complete the Second Amendment and NRA questionnaire that follows and then go to the Meaning of Test Results section at the end of the book to get a better idea of where you stand on the gun-control issue.

Key Quotation of Chapter 2

... It is time we get on with the business of treating guns with the respect they require and one small step toward that end is making it clear that regulating gun ownership does not violate the Constitution.

—R. William Ide, President, American Bar Association

THE SECOND AMENDMENT AND NRA QUESTIONNAIRE

Please indicate your level of agreement with each of the following statements.

1 = strongly disagree, 2 = disagree, 3 = undecided, 4 = agree, and 5 = strongly agree.

1. _____ The Second Amendment guarantees all law-abiding citizens the right to bear arms.

2. _____ The National Guard is the United States' well-regulated militia.

3. _____ The Second Amendment is an individual right.

4. _____ The Second Amendment should be revised to make it appropriate to the twenty-first century.

5. _____ The Second Amendment is a collective right.

6. _____ The Second Amendment does not include servants, slaves, vagabonds, and women.

7. _____ The original intent of the NRA was "to promote and encourage rifle shooting on a scientific basis."

8. _____ Since its inception, the NRA has opposed all gun-control measures.

9. _____ I would like to be a member of the NRA.

10. _____ The NRA is interested in the welfare of law-abiding citizens.

You can review your results by going to the Meaning of Test Results section at the end of the book.

3

Assassinations and Attempted Assassinations of Presidents, An Ex-President, and Presidential Candidates

Guns Are Fun

See that living legend over there?
With one little squeeze of the trigger
I can put that person at my feet moaning
and groaning and pleading with God
This gun gives me pornographic power.
If I wish, the President will fall
and the world would look at me in disbelief
all because I own an inexpensive gun.[1]

—John W. Hinckley Jr.

- Did you know that four United States presidents were assassinated—three with handguns and one with a rifle?

- Did you know that assassination attempts have been made against five other presidents—all but one with handguns or an assault rifle?

- Did you know that two assassination attempts were made with handguns on one president?

- Did you know that an assassination attempt was made with a handgun on an ex-president?

19

- Did you know that one presidential candidate was assassinated with a handgun?

- Did you know that an assassination attempt was made with a handgun on a presidential candidate?

- Did you know that, over the past forty-odd years, one president and one presidential candidate were assassinated, and assassination attempts were made against three other presidents and one presidential candidate?

- *Are you outraged by these truths?*

Before we discuss the assassinations and attempted assassinations of American politicians, it is important for you to understand that even before the Constitution was ratified, guns were used by evil men to assassinate or attempt to assassinate public figures. For example, in 1776, Thomas Hickey, a personal bodyguard of the governor of New York, attempted to kidnap and assassinate General George Washington. He was found guilty of treason and publicly hanged before twenty thousand spectators.

During this period, it also was quite common for men to solve conflicts by challenging their adversaries to duels. This also was true for politicians. Perhaps the most famous duel occurred in 1804 between Aaron Burr and Alexander Hamilton. Burr was Thomas Jefferson's vice president. Hamilton, the first secretary of the treasury, had made many scurrilous statements about Burr and opposed his nomination to be governor of New York. Burr challenged Hamilton to a duel, and Hamilton accepted. As the person being challenged, Hamilton was the one to choose the weapons, and he chose dueling pistols. Hamilton had rigged the pistols, but his fired before he could take careful aim. Burr then killed Hamilton—with a handgun. Some members of the general public expressed outrage.[2] A crowd soon gathered near Burr's home, chanting:

> Oh Burr, Oh Burr, What hast thou done,
> Thou hast shooted dead great Hamilton!
> You hid behind a bunch of thistle
> And shooted him dead with a great hoss pistol![3]

Reverend Lyman Beecher's sermons denounced dueling, characterizing it as a great national sin. He asserted that if the majority of eligible voters voted against dueling politicians, "The practice of fighting duels [would] speedily cease."[4] Unfortunately, duels were still used thereafter to resolve many conflicts, and no great pushes for gun legislation were attempted as a result of the Burr-Hamilton duel. As recently as the 2004 presidential election, Senator Zell Miller (D-GA) challenged Chris Matthews, host of the television show "Hardball," to a duel.

ATTEMPTED ASSASSINATION OF PRESIDENT ANDREW JACKSON

On January 30, 1835, Richard Lawrence, an unemployed and deranged house painter, attempted to assassinate President Andrew Jackson with two handguns as Jackson left the chamber of the House of Representatives. Lawrence fired two derringers at Jackson, but both misfired.[5] Jackson responded by chasing Lawrence and beating him over the head with his cane. Lawrence spent the remainder of his life in an asylum.

The general public was upset by the assassination attempt, but this had no impact on the gun-control issue. In part, this might have been due to the fact that Jackson was known for his dueling skills. Jackson's most famous duel had been against Charles Dickerson, a young lawyer who had apparently slandered Jackson's wife, and Jackson had killed Dickinson. As Alexander DeConde writes regarding this duel, "Locals in Nashville, Tennessee, treated their confrontation as a sporting event, making bets on its outcome."[6]

ASSASSINATION OF PRESIDENT ABRAHAM LINCOLN

Abraham Lincoln was shot in the head at point-blank range with a single-shot derringer on April 14, 1865, as he was watching *Our American Cousin* in Ford's Theater in Washington, D.C. He died the following day. John Wilkes Booth, a southerner and well known Shakespearian actor, had hated Lincoln for freeing the slaves. He had been outraged by one of Lincoln's speeches, in which the president had suggested that voting rights should be granted to certain blacks. After shooting President Lincoln, Booth fled the scene on horseback. Federal authorities chased him and caught up with him at Richard Garrett's farm near Port Royal, Virginia, on April 26. Authorities set the barn in which Booth had been hiding on fire, but Booth refused to surrender and was shot to death by Sergeant Boston Corbett.[7]

At the end of the Civil War, General Ulysses S. Grant permitted Confederate officers and Union soldiers to retain their firearms. Nationalists believed that gun ownership made citizens more patriotic. Lincoln's assassination did not cause the general public to clamor for gun legislation. Rather, it seemed to advance the proliferation of guns in the United States during the 1870s and 1880s.[8]

ASSASSINATION OF PRESIDENT JAMES A. GARFIELD

On July 2, 1881, Charles J. Guiteau shot President James A. Garfield at the railroad station in Washington, D.C. He used an English caliber pistol to shoot the president. He shot twice; one bullet hit the president's arm, but the other found its mark and lodged in his chest. Garfield lived for another eighty days, dying on September 19, 1881.[9]

Guiteau had worked to get Garfield elected and believed that he deserved to be appointed to a consul-generalship in Vienna. Guiteau later stated that he "… never had the slightest doubt as to the Divine inspiration of the act, and it was for the best interest of the American people."[10] He had been considered mildly deranged and exceedingly depraved by Garfield's staff. He was executed.

After Garfield's assassination, anti-gun editorials appeared in newspapers, and the United States courts discouraged citizens from brandishing guns. Some cities and states enacted gun-control laws. Journalists wrote disapprovingly about individuals carrying concealed weapons. Some journalists believed that "individuals carrying concealed small firearms" were a "prime contributor to the spread of deadly violence" and that "… without ready access to cheap guns the criminal class could not kill with ease."[11]

Gun control advocates are still saying this today. Garfield's assassination had advanced the case for gun control. The NRA was not active in the gun debate that followed Garfield's assassination.

ASSASSINATION OF PRESIDENT WILLIAM McKINLEY

On September 6, 1901, at the Pan-American Exposition in Buffalo, New York, President William McKinley was shot by Leon Czolgosz with a short-barreled,

.32 caliber Iver-Johnson revolver, which he had concealed with a handkerchief. McKinley died on September 14. Czolgosz, a twenty-eight-year-old son of a Polish immigrant and self-proclaimed anarchist, claimed that he had shot McKinley "because he was the enemy of the good people—the good working people. I am not sorry for my crime."[12] He claimed that he had only done his duty. He was tried and executed. The assassination, however, did not trigger an outcry for gun-control legislation.[13]

After McKinley's assassination, Theodore Roosevelt became president. He was an avid hunter, a sportsman who promoted shooting at gun clubs, and a member of the NRA. In 1905, however, gun owners came under greater scrutiny. DeConde asserts: "The Kansas Supreme Court held that the constitutional right to bear arms applied only to members of state militias in their official capacity while in actual service. It conferred only a collective right to own arms."[14] The United States Congress, however, supported the individual theory of the right to own arms. In 1906, the NRA allowed women to become members, and it continued to nurture its credibility with Congress and the American public. McKinley's assassination did not produce any federal gun legislation.

ATTEMPTED ASSASSINATION OF EX-PRESIDENT THEODORE ROOSEVELT

On October 14, 1912, John Schrank shot Theodore Roosevelt in the right side of his chest while he was campaigning in Milwaukee as a candidate for the Bull Moose Party. Schrank, a psychotic New York saloonkeeper, shot Roosevelt with a .38 caliber pistol. The gun had been aimed at Roosevelt's head, but a bystander had seen it and had deflected the bullet by pushing Schrank's arm. Roosevelt responded to the shooting by saying that "I have been shot, but it takes more than that to kill a Bull Moose."[15] Roosevelt believed that a person had a constitutional right to defend himself with firearms. In fact, Roosevelt often talked about how he would defend himself if someone were to attempt to kill him. When discussing what he would have done in the late President McKinley's place, he said that he would have shot back. He claimed that he held no animosity toward Schrank. Instead, he suggested that Schrank should be held responsible for his attempt to kill him. Schrank was sent to a state hospital where he remained until he died in 1943.

ATTEMPTED ASSASSINATION OF PRESIDENT FRANKLIN D. ROOSEVELT

On February 15, 1933, Giuseppe Zangara, a thirty-two-year-old bricklayer, attempted to assassinate President Franklin D. Roosevelt in Miami. Zangara had purchased a .32 caliber revolver at a local pawnshop for eight dollars.[16] He shot five times but missed Roosevelt. The bullets struck five bystanders, including Anton J. Cermak, the mayor of Chicago, who died a few weeks later as a result of his wound. Zangara claimed that he didn't hate Roosevelt personally. He said, "I hate all Presidents, no matter from what country they come, and I hate all officials and everybody who is rich."[17]

The shooting spree and attempted assassination of President Roosevelt shocked the nation. As a result, the issue of gun control was thrust upon federal lawmakers. According to Carl Bakal, thousands of Americans wrote letters to their congressmen urging the immediate prohibition of the interstate sale of pistols.

On March 2, 1933, Judge Uly O. Thompson of the Eleventh Judicial Circuit Court of Florida confirmed Zangara's conviction. Before sentencing him to eighty years in prison, Thompson stated:

> Three presidents of the United States have been assassinated. We have had just a few more than thirty presidents, so that out of every ten, one has been killed, so far, by an assassin. One other ex-president was shot in a public appearance … These assassinations have either been perfected or undertaken by a man armed with a pistol, and yet the people of this country steadfastly permit the manufacture, sale, and possession of such deadly and useless weapons. I say "useless" for this reason: A pistol in the hands of an assassin is sure death and murder, while a pistol in the hands of you good people and the good people of this country is about the most useless weapon of defense with which you can arm yourself.[18]

After Mayor Cermak died on March 6, Zangara was retried and sentenced to death. On March 20 Zangara died in the electric chair at Florida State Penitentiary for the murder of Chicago Mayor Anton Cermak.

Unlike prior presidents, Franklin D. Roosevelt supported federal gun legislation. In part, this might have been a result of having served as assistant secretary of the navy and on the executive committee of the National Crime Commission. When he was governor of New York, he had supported restrictive state handgun controls. He had also argued with Karl Frederick, the president of the NRA, about the control of handguns. Frederick protested vehemently against the idea of provisions for fingerprinting citizens who purchase handguns, stating that this was against the Second Amendment of the Constitution. Frederick employed the NRA's frequently used comparison between automobile deaths and handgun deaths. He stated that, "Automobile owners, though not fingerprinted, were as a class a much more criminal body, from the standpoint of percentage, than pistol licensees."[19] He admitted, however, that he had no statistical data to support his claim. The NRA, through the pages of *American Rifleman,* attempted to persuade its members and those of other hunting organizations to write letters and send telegrams to their congressmen. An advertisement in the magazine claimed that law-enforcement officials and congressmen were pushing for the registration of all firearms, whereas the proposed bill in fact excluded rifles and shotguns.

The letters and telegrams sent by NRA members persuaded many legislators not to vote for gun-control laws. The majority of congressmen, however, were not swayed by the NRA and were successful in passing the first federal gun con-trol bill—the National Firearms Act of 1934. The act imposed a tax on the man-ufacture or transfer of gangster-type weapons, requiring that they be registered with the Treasury Department. These weapons included machine guns, subma-chine guns, and all other fully automatic weapons. The act did not apply to pis-tols and revolvers, ordinary sporting or target-type rifles, or shotguns. The amended bill was quite different from the one first proposed by Attorney General Homer Cummings. According to the original proposal, pistols and revolvers were to be registered with the Treasury Department. Nevertheless, even though the bill had been watered down, it represented the first partial victory for federal gun-control advocates. Finally, gun-control advocates had scored in the gun game.[20]

ATTEMPTED ASSASSINATION OF PRESIDENT HARRY S TRUMAN

On November 1, 1950, Oscar Collazo and Griselio Torresola, two Puerto Rican nationalists, tried to assassinate President Harry S Truman at Blair House in Washington, D.C. Collazo and Torresola used German 9 mm automatic guns to shoot their way into the building, which is the president's official state guest house and was being used as Truman's residence while the White House was being renovated. At the time of the break-in, Truman was taking a nap inside. The would-be assassins wounded three White House policemen. One of the wounded policemen, Leslie Coffelt, shot Torresola in the head, killing him instantly. Collazo was captured, tried, convicted, and sentenced to death. One week before Collazo's scheduled execution, Truman commuted his sentence to life imprisonment.[21]

ASSASSINATION OF PRESIDENT JOHN F. KENNEDY

On November 22, 1963, President John F. Kennedy was assassinated by Lee Harvey Oswald in Dallas, Texas. Oswald used an Italian Mannlicher-Carcano carbine fitted with a four-power telescopic sight to kill the president. Oswald had used a coupon from *American Rifleman* to purchase the rifle from a mail-order house in Chicago for $19.95.[22] Oswald was later killed by Jack Ruby before he could be tried.

Not until the assassination of President Kennedy did a significant percentage of the public begin to clamor against the sale of guns to criminals, juveniles, and the mentally ill. Carl Bakal states: "To many people, indeed, it seemed that such legislation was long overdue. Within the last one hundred years, bullets had aimed at seven presidents and killed four of the thirty-five presidents—a record perhaps unparalleled in the annals of history."[23] The general public responded to the assassination by writing letters, sending telegrams, and making telephone calls to their congressmen with demands for immediate gun-control laws.

An editorial in the *Washington Post* on November 27, 1963, pointed out that television had conveyed powerfully the tragedy of the assassination. Because schools and many businesses were closed after the assassination, approximately one hundred million people watched the tragic results of what a gun can do in the hands of a criminal.[24] In addition, millions of Americans witnessed the assassination of Lee Harvey Oswald. Many members of Congress spoke out about the president's tragic death. Representative John Lindsay (R-NY) seemed to echo the feelings of the public when he said that the tragedy had created a sense of brotherhood among the people of the world. This might be comparable to the intense sense of community felt by many immediately after the 9/11 tragedy.

Senator Thomas Dodd (D-CT), a longtime leading advocate for gun control, felt as though he held a lit fuse in his hand. Rather than use the fuse to simply pass bill S.1975, which prohibited the mail-order sale of pistols, he amended it to cover all firearms. But Kennedy's assassination caused much confusion among members of Congress, and this confusion dissipated any chance of immediate legislation.[25] One factor that appeared favorable for gun-control advocates was that *American Rifleman*'s most recent issue had been published just before Kennedy's assassination, and, thus, the NRA was unable to respond immediately to the tragedy or to ask its members to write letters to their congressmen opposing gun legislation.

Although the NRA initially gave lip service to the original bill (S.1975) after Kennedy's assassination—perhaps in deference to public opinion or perhaps because of a sense of responsibility—it soon sent out bulletins to affiliates stating that it did not support any federal gun-control laws. It appeared, however, that Franklin L. Orth, the executive vice president of the NRA, had been emotionally touched by the tragedy. He at first supported the original Dodd bill, but he later rescinded this support after receiving several threatening phone calls.

The NRA published an editorial in *American Rifleman* in December, 1963 stating that:

> One is forever being told that you don't have to protect yourself—that is the job of the police. What type of talk is this for Americans? Are we becoming a nation of defeatists, devoid of personal pride and content to rely entirely on our police for protection?[26]

Other articles and editorials also stressed that if you want to be a man, you must know how to protect your family and yourself. The NRA again appeared to be motivated by a dollar-and-cents type of logic with strong admixtures of pseudopatriotism to promote their status.

The arguments between the NRA and gun-control groups continued through December of 1963. During the first four months of 1964, a great number of congressmen and law-enforcement officials joined the fight for gun control. Congressman Lindsay, in his testimony before the Senate Commerce Committee, stated:

> Responsible sportsmen and gun owners find their sport or hobby degraded by the greedy practice of gun buyers. I cannot see how it helps bona fide hunters, gun lovers, and even dealers and manufacturers to have a national sport become a national scandal.[27]

Senator Dodd, a strong advocate for federal gun-control legislation, posed the following question: "What general good is guaranteed by allowing men and children to possess firearms in secret?" Dodd amended bill S.1975 twice to include rifles and shotguns and to require dealers to have their licenses authenticated by senior law-enforcement officials. He also posed another question: "What more do we need than the death of a beloved President to arouse us to place some regulation on the traffic of guns for crime?"[28]

The NRA was unable to answer Dodd's questions satisfactorily. Orth stated that the NRA was considering a reexamination of pistol procedures for assuring its members and the public that purchasers are "citizens of good repute."[29] An article in the *New York Times* on December 8, 1964, also supported the idea that the NRA was concerned about the public demand for gun laws and that some NRA members empathized with gun-control advocates.

> The differences that have developed within the NRA are perhaps the best testimony to the growing public demand for effective control of traffic in firearms. It seems obvious that the association would not have accepted a change in its traditional opposition to any such legislation if they had not been convinced that acceptance of minor reforms was their best hope.[30]

The editorial also stated that many NRA members felt a need for federal gun control laws. This was a temporary conviction, however, for they soon returned to the traditional arguments that they had employed since the 1920s. The gun lobby claimed that the Second Amendment of the Constitution guaranteed all law-abiding citizens the "right to bear arms," that the real man knows how to defend himself with a gun, that automobiles kill more people than guns and should be outlawed before guns, and that those advocating gun legislation are part of a conspiracy to disarm America that would ultimately leave the people helpless.

Kennedy's assassination helped to focus the debate on the need for federal gun-control legislation, and the debate has continued to this day.

ASSASSINATION OF PRESIDENTIAL CANDIDATE ROBERT F. KENNEDY

On June 5, 1968, Sirhan Bishara Sirhan, a Jordanian immigrant, shot Senator Robert F. Kennedy with a .22 caliber pistol at the Ambassador Hotel in Los Angeles. Kennedy died on June 6 at the Good Samaritan Hospital. Sirhan had wanted to kill Kennedy because the senator had supported Israel in the Six Day War. On March 3, 1969, in a Los Angeles courtroom, Sirhan confessed that he had killed Kennedy. He was sentenced to death, but the sentence was commuted to life in prison in 1972.[31]

President Lyndon Johnson, in response to this latest Kennedy tragedy, stated on nationwide television that Congress should not settle for a halfway measure concerning gun-control laws. He stressed that America must have the gun control it needed:

> I call upon the nation in the name of sanity. I call upon the Congress in the name of safety and in the name of an ordered citizenship to give America the gun control laws that America needs.... So let us spell out our grief in constructive action.[32]

Senator Dodd announced that he was going to submit a bill requiring registration of all firearms. In addition, various media outlets, including the *New York Times* and *Washington Post*, became active in pushing for gun laws by chastising the NRA and its dollars-and-cents logic.

The battle between gun-control and gun-rights groups continued throughout 1968. Despite the opposition of the NRA and congressmen who supported the organization, the Omnibus Crime Bill and Safe Streets Acts were passed in June of 1968. The silent majority of Americans can be credited with having put sufficient pressure on Congress to ensure the bills' passage.

ATTEMPTED ASSASSINATION OF PRESIDENTIAL CANDIDATE GEORGE WALLACE

On May 15, 1972, at a shopping center in Laurel, Maryland, Arthur Bremer attempted to assassinate presidential candidate Governor George Wallace (D-AL). Prior to shooting Wallace, Bremer had concealed his .38 caliber revolver in his pocket. He pulled out the revolver and shot Wallace five times. Wallace survived, but he was paralyzed from the waist down for the remainder of his life. Bremer did not have a criminal record, and so he had been able to go to Casanova Guns and purchase the .38 caliber revolver and a 9 mm Browning automatic.[33]

At Bremer's trial, the defense attorney argued that Bremer was a schizophrenic and psychotic. Bremer had indicated in his diary that his intent had been apolitical. He had said that he wanted to "do something bold and dramatic, forcefull and dynamic, a statement of my manhood for the world to see."[34] The judge sentenced him to sixty-three years in a Maryland state penitentiary. He is due to be released in 2025.

After the passage of the Gun Control Act of 1968, both the gun-control and NRA lobbies continued to fight for their viewpoints. After Wallace was shot, the Gun Control Registration and Licensing Act of 1971 received more attention. Senator Edward Kennedy—whose two brothers had been assassinated during the previous decade—called the bill a model to begin curbing widespread violence caused by the misuse of guns. Alexander DeConde wrote that President Richard Nixon "always felt there was a need for federal handgun legislation."[35] Nixon believed that the "Saturday night special" should be controlled and indicated that he would sign a bill to support such controls. Congressman John W. Murphy (D-NY) described firearm owners as "gun nuts" who "think their weapons are extensions of their penises."[36] The NRA argued for controlling crime rather than forcing law-abiding citizens to register their handguns. Nixon did not push for additional gun legislation. Thus, no significant gun legislation was passed in the aftermath of the Wallace assassination attempt.

ATTEMPTED ASSASSINATION OF PRESIDENT GERALD R. FORD

On September 5, 1975, Lynette Alice "Squeaky" Fromme pointed an unloaded .45 caliber Colt automatic pistol at President Gerald R. Ford in Sacramento, California. Fromme had been a member of Charles Manson's murderous "family."[37] Seventeen days later, on September 22, 1975, Sara Jane Moore, a maladjusted FBI informant, also tried to kill President Ford. As he entered the Saint Francis Hotel in San Francisco, she attempted to fire a .38 caliber Smith and Wesson revolver at him. Both women were convicted of attempted murder and sentenced to life in prison.[38]

After the passage of the Gun Control Act of 1968, the NRA continued to cite its traditional themes: "All law-abiding citizens have the right to bear arms" and "Guns don't kill people; people kill people." The NRA continued to oppose gun legislation in both houses of Congress and was successful in helping to defeat Senator Joseph Clark (D-PA) and Senator Joseph Tydings (D-MD), two powerful gun-control advocates. President Ford, however, did not push for gun legislation and received the backing of the NRA in the 1976 presidential election.

ATTEMPTED ASSASSINATION OF PRESIDENT RONALD REAGAN

On March 30, 1981, outside the Washington Hilton Hotel, John W. Hinckley Jr., a mentally disturbed young man, attempted to kill President Ronald Reagan with a handgun. Hinckley shot Reagan just below the heart, and Reagan was rushed to the George Washington Hospital, where he underwent surgery to remove the bullet, which had entered his lung. Hinckley also seriously wounded a Secret Service agent and shot James Brady, Reagan's press secretary, in the head. Deconde writes: "... he used a gun because he knew it as the most deadly concealable weapon at hand."[39] Hinckley did not appear to have had a deep-seated hatred for President Reagan, but he had been obsessed with a young actress, Jodie Foster, and had wanted to impress her by killing the president.

Hinckley had easily obtained his pistol. He had merely walked into a pawnshop in Dallas, Texas, and for twenty-nine dollars had purchased an RG-14, .22 caliber revolver made in Germany. Sarah Brady, the wife of James Brady, later became a spokesperson for the gun-control movement. She stated:

> The case of John Hinckley is a vivid reminder of how easy it is for a handgun to fall into the wrong hands. He walked into a Dallas pawnshop, purchased a cheap 'Saturday night special'—no questions asked, no waiting period to see if he had a criminal or mental illness record—and a minute later was on his way, ready to shoot the president of the United States.[40]

This quotation appears in *Guns, Crime and Freedom* by Wayne LaPierre, executive vice-president of the National Rifle Association. In this book, he concludes: "No waiting period ever devised would have stopped Hinckley. The passage of ... [a law mandating a waiting] period would only be a 'symbolic victory.'"[41] A waiting period, according to LaPierre, would lead to government intrusion into the lives of law-abiding citizens. He pointed out that Hinckley had had no criminal record and no committal for mental illness or incompetence. Therefore, Hinckley had met the requirement of a law-abiding citizen and, thus, met the requirement to purchase a handgun.

LaPierre did not discuss the facts that, since the beginning of the twentieth century, two presidents had been assassinated, four attempts had been made to assassinate presidents, one former president had been shot, one presidential candidate had been shot, and one presidential candidate had been assassinated. LaPierre was only concerned that law-abiding citizens be allowed to purchase guns without a long waiting period. His logic could be expressed in the following way:

> John Hinckley is a law-abiding citizen.
> Law-abiding citizens should be allowed to purchase guns.
> Therefore, John Hinckley should be allowed to purchase a gun.

When John Hinckley becomes a lawless citizen, he should then no longer be able to purchase a gun. And so, following LaPierre's logic, all law-abiding citizens should be allowed to purchase a gun, even if their intent is to attempt to assassinate the president.

Unfortunately, after President Reagan recovered from his surgery, he refused to change his mind about gun laws. He said in his first news conference after returning to work that focusing on gun control would divert attention from trying "to solve the crime problem." He also claimed that gun control laws were "virtually unenforceable."[42]

This same defeatist attitude has permeated the gun issue for the past eighty years. Mr. Reagan had an opportunity to become a leader for federal gun legislation. Instead, he suggested without foundation that federal gun control legislation would be unenforceable.

Fortunately, since James Brady was shot in the head, he and his wife, Sarah, have focused on gun control issues. Their efforts persuaded Ronald Reagan to sign the Undetectable Firearms Act into law in 1988.

ATTEMPTED ASSASSINATION OF PRESIDENT BILL CLINTON

On October 29, 1994, Francisco Duran fired shots at the White House. He used a Chinese-made 7.62 mm semiautomatic rifle. Duran, an upholsterer, allegedly fired twenty-nine rounds at the White House, striking it several times. He was charged with four counts of assault on four Secret Service agents and two counts of illegal possession of a firearm by a convicted felon, as well as other charges. He was sentenced to life in prison.

Mr. Clinton had supported strong gun-control laws prior to the attempted assassination in 1994. In fact, the Democratic platform in 1992 had supported strong gun-control measures, including a waiting period for handgun purchases, "a ban of the most deadly assault weapons," and swift punishment for crimes committed with guns. Clinton had also supported the Brady Bill.[43] In contrast, the Republican platform of 1992 had opposed the Brady Bill and had repeatedly stated that it supported the "right to bear arms." Throughout his presidency, Clinton was a supporter and friend of gun-control advocates.[44]

Conclusion

Four American presidents have been assassinated—two in the nineteenth century and two in the twentieth century. There have also been an assassination attempt on a president in the nineteenth century and six assassination attempts on presidents in the twentieth century. In addition, one presidential candidate was assassinated, and another candidate was shot five times. In 1966, Bakal asserted that this is "a record perhaps unparalleled in the annals of history."[45]

Although a small percentage of the general public expressed outrage over dueling and the assassinations of Presidents Lincoln and Garfield in the nineteenth century, it was not until the attempted assassination of Franklin D. Roosevelt and the assassinations of President John F. Kennedy, Dr. Martin Luther King Jr., and Senator Robert F. Kennedy that the general public—the silent majority—expressed their outrage and demanded federal gun legislation.

Since 1968, attempts have been made to assassinate Presidents Ford, Reagan and Clinton. Fortunately, these attempts failed. It is common knowledge that President George W. Bush has hundreds of Secret Service agents to protect him from assassination attempts, and this protection will continue for future Presidents. Future gun-control legislation might reduce the dangers of gun violence against our political leaders. As you will learn in the next two chapters, federal gun-control advocates have had some successes in the gun games, but, for the most part, the NRA is still winning most of the gun games.

I have not created a closed-ended questionnaire for this chapter, but please reflect on the following open-ended questions:

- Why do Republican Presidents not support federal gun-control legislation?

- Why do Democratic Presidents support federal gun-control legislation?

- Do you support federal gun legislation? Why or why not?

Key Quotation of Chapter 3

I call upon the nation in the name of sanity. I call upon the Congress in the name of safety and in the name of an ordered citizenship to give America the gun control laws that America needs.... So let us spell out our grief in constructive action.

—President Lyndon B. Johnson

4

Gun Movements from 1922 through 1968

There is a gun crisis in the United States. Between 1933 and 1982, nearly one million Americans were killed with firearms.[1]

—Violence Policy Center

Ours is the most violent society. The United States rates the highest in violence among industrial countries. We have ten times the murder rate of Great Britain. We have eight times the rate of Japan, and five times that of Germany and France. The reason is that when we assault, we assault with guns, and guns kill.[2]

—James M. Hester

In the spring of 1922, a little less than four years after the signing of the armistice with Germany, a concerted attempt was made by lawmakers to enact federal gun-control legislation. The proposed legislation was intended primarily to prohibit the sale of handguns to criminals, the mentally ill, and juveniles. At the time, however, a majority of congressmen opposed federal firearm legislation because they thought it would be "infringing upon the people's rights." The lawmakers justified their position based on their interpretation of the Constitution. This interpretation was supported by the National Rifle Association (NRA), the Ku Klux Klan (KKK), and a majority of the public.

This chapter discusses the various gun movements of specific periods: 1922–1927, 1934–1938, 1947, 1957, 1958–1962, and 1963–1968. As you read about these movements, think about the following questions:

- Why did the NRA and pro-gun congressmen oppose federal gun legislation during the nineteen twenties?

- Why did the NRA oppose federal gun legislation after the assassination attempt on President Franklin D. Roosevelt?

- Why did the NRA oppose federal gun legislation that focused on keeping guns out of the hands of juveniles?

- Why did the NRA oppose stamping guns with serial numbers?

- Why did the NRA oppose the registration of firearms?

- Why did the NRA oppose licensing handgun owners?

- How could the NRA not support banning mail-order guns after Lee Harvey Oswald used one to kill President John F. Kennedy?

- Why would the NRA not support federal gun legislation after Dr. Martin Luther King and Senator Robert F. Kennedy were assassinated?

- Why did the NRA continually lie in *American Rifleman* about gun-control advocates from the 1920s through the 1960s?

As you read this chapter, make your own assessment about who is winning the gun game.

1922–1927 GUN MOVEMENT

The years following World War I presented the public with an opportunity to acquire inexpensive guns. The rates of gun violence and murder increased significantly in the United States during the early 1920s. This caused police chiefs, judges, and special committees of the American Bar Association to express their views, through newspaper editorials and magazine articles, about the need for federal gun-control laws. Likewise, using the same media, many members of the NRA and the general public who opposed gun legislation also expressed their viewpoints.

Several editorials published in the *New York Times* argued the need for federal handgun legislation. One editorial published in December 1923 asserted: "The sale of weapons should be carefully regulated. The problem is one of how to keep them out of the hands of man killers. No one has yet found a solution for it."[3] The editorial was strengthened by the use of statistics related to the increased number of murders committed annually in the United States. It was determined by the FBI that, of the ten thousand murders committed annually as a result of firearms, 90 percent were committed with handguns.[4]

Two years later, in September 1925 an editorial was published in the *Times* that acknowledged the increase of crime and murder involving guns, but did not suggest a solution to the problem: "That the proposed prohibition of manufacture and sale of firearms and ammunition save for regulating official purposes has much practical value may be doubted. The gunman will hardly lack a gun. This is necessary in his business."[5] This editorial sympathized with congressmen and law-enforcement officials who supported federal gun-control laws, but it simultaneously attempted to refute the idealistic notion that such laws would be workable in our society. Two days after this editorial appeared, the *Times* reported that many law-enforcement officials believed that if the manufacturers of pistols, revolvers, and similar firearms were absolutely stopped, it would be possible to disarm the criminal population.[6] It, however, also would result in disarming law-abiding citizens, which was not the goal of federal gun-control laws. Thus, the NRA won the gun game.

Like the United States, post–World War I Great Britain also experienced a surge in crime. Unlike the United States, Britain modified its gun laws by revisiting its 1903 Pistol Act. After a lively debate in Parliament between the pro-gun group and gun-control supporters, the House of Commons passed the Firearms Act of 1920 by a vote of 254 to 6. The Act was designed "to prevent criminals and persons of that description from being able to have revolvers and to use them."[7] In essence, it repealed the legal privilege of civilians to keep handguns. In Britain's case, the gun-control group won the gun game.

1934–1938 GUN MOVEMENT

As mentioned in Chapter 3, Giuseppe Zangara attempted to assassinate Franklin D. Roosevelt in 1933 with a handgun in Miami. As a result, the House Ways and Means Committee of the Seventy-Third Congress became more active in researching the gun issue. The committee discovered that guns were continuing to flow into the country in unrestricted numbers, not only to criminal mobs but to the entire population. The number of homicides, suicides, and accidents attributed to firearms had increased by 80 percent between 1920 and 1933.[8]

Attorney General Homer Cummings reported to the committee that 75 percent of firearm murders were committed with concealable weapons. He argued the need for legislation. His bill (HR 9066) required that "... all manufacturers, dealers, importers, and pawnbrokers dealing in firearms ... pay an annual occupational tax, and ... keep records of all their transactions. Firearms were defined to mean pistols, revolvers, and such 'gangster weapons' as machine guns and rifles...." HR 9066 required that each weapon be registered and that a tax be levied on its transfer. A weapon's new owner would be identified by fingerprinting and a photograph, among other information. A related bill provided for the regulation of the sale of ammunition.[9]

Cummings argued that his bill was necessary because crime had mushroomed during the previous decade. He said that approximately five hundred thousand lawless persons "are carrying about with them, or have available at hand, weapons of the most deadly character."[10] Karl Frederick, president of the NRA, objected to the registration of pistols and revolvers, as well as fingerprinting, because he claimed these procedures went against the Second Amendment. NRA members responded to the proposed law by sending letters and telegrams to their congressmen.

Provisions of the National Firearms Act of 1934 were:

- A tax on the manufacture, sale, and transfer of sawed-off shotguns, sawed-off rifles, machine guns, and silencers.

- A requirement that the purchasers of these weapons undergo FBI background checks and get approval from local law-enforcement officers.[11]

The act did not apply to pistols and revolvers, ordinary sporting or target-type rifles and shotguns, or ammunition. The act was quite different than the one proposed by Cummings. In the original proposal, pistols and revolvers had to be registered with the Treasury Department, dealers had to pay an occupational tax, and owners of all weapons had to be fingerprinted and photographed. Cummings's bill had been watered down to the point at which it was questionable whether gun-control advocates had won any type of victory at all. In the end, it appeared as though the NRA had scored more points than had the gun-control advocates. The NRA won that gun game.

Cummings continued to voice his opinions between 1934 and 1938. In 1937, before the House Ways and Means Committee, he questioned the character of those opposed to strict gun-control legislation:

> No honest man can object to registration, a procedure much simpler than the registration and licensing procedure applicable to automobiles. Show me a

man who doesn't want his gun registered, and I will show you a man who shouldn't have a gun.[12]

Bakal writes that this considerably upset hunting organizations, who claimed that the statement was unpatriotic, and NRA members believed that their inalienable rights as protected by the Constitution were being attacked. Cummings continued to fight, citing updated statistics and facts that were not refuted by the NRA. He had also gained the support of the International Association of Police. *American Rifleman,* however, castigated the efforts of Cummings and other federal gun-control supporters:

> Once again, the members of the National Rifle Association will need to be represented by their officers in pointing out to Congress the hidden dangers of such a plausible legislative scheme to end crime. Once again we ask every active member to use this coupon to say, "The right of the American citizen to bear arms shall not be infringed."[13]

With the support of the NRA, pro-gun congressmen put pressure on Cummings, and he was forced to compromise in order to get any legislation passed at all.

The Federal Firearms Act of 1938:

- Required annual licenses for manufacturers, dealers, and importers of firearms and handgun ammunition.

- Banned known criminals from owning firearms.[14]

The bill had many shortcomings, for nothing in it could prevent a criminal from acquiring a gun through the mail.

The passage of this weak bill thwarted the efforts of Cummings, and the movement soon came to an end. The NRA had used its traditional letter-writing tactics to defeat the gun-control advocates. In part, the NRA was successful because President Roosevelt had not himself pushed for stronger gun-control legislation. Thus, the NRA had won another round in the gun game.

1947 GUN MOVEMENT

In 1947, a third gun movement began to develop when Attorney General Thomas Clark requested that Senator Alexander Wiley (D-WI), the chair of the Senate Judiciary Committee, introduce legislation that would prohibit ownership of firearms by juveniles, strengthen importation laws so that criminals could not easily acquire guns, and prevent United States soldiers from bringing guns home from abroad. Wiley presented several reasons why federal gun control laws were needed. He stated that a large number of small arms were unaccounted for by the armed forces, that a considerable number of them had been found in the possession of members of the underworld, and that, during the previous year, five hundred thousand crimes had been committed by minors, the majority of them with firearms.[15]

The NRA's propaganda wheels were once again set into motion against the proposed bill, which the group called an attempt "to revive the idea of Gestapo-type Federal firearms registration law."[16] At first, Senator Wiley attempted to refute the traditional arguments of the NRA, but he was unsuccessful. The NRA, again, had won the gun game.

1957 GUN MOVEMENT

Another decade passed before an attempt was made by the Internal Revenue Service (IRS) to strengthen the 1938 Firearm Act. This act had outlawed the traffic of any firearms "from which the manufacturer's serial number had been removed, obliterated, or altered."[17] The proposed change required all manufacturers and importers of guns to stamp each of them with a serial number. Another addition required a person to sign his/her name when purchasing a firearm or ammunition for a pistol. In order to implement these changes to the act, many aggressive speakers, including James L Sullivan, chief counsel for the Senate Subcommittee on Juvenile Delinquency, and Leroy E. Wike, executive secretary of the International Association of Chiefs of Police, gave their support.[18]

Sullivan believed that the IRS proposals would keep firearms out of the hands of the criminal element, the mentally unbalanced, and juveniles, who in the past year had used pistols in 42 percent of their crimes. Wike reinforced Sullivan's remarks and suggested that:

> ... the average person who likes to own and use a fine firearm should not object to an acceptable means of positively identifying the piece when he registers no objection to the manufacturer's name, serial number, and type of product on his television, camera, radio, air conditioner, and outboard motor, his wife's food mixer, electric range, garbage disposal or any of the dozen mechanisms necessary for modern living.[19]

Many NRA members and like-minded congressmen did not attempt to refute the charges of the IRS, but rather simply reasserted the traditional arguments based on the constitutional phrase, "the right to bear arms shall not be infringed."[20]

James H. Holton, who represented the Veterans of Foreign Wars, castigated gun-control advocates by stating, "We must not shut our eyes to the fact that there are, in this country, subversive elements which desire a police state."[21] He continued: "We Believe That the Ultimate Defender of His Personal Liberty Is an Angry and Resolute Free Man, Armed with a Firearm."[22] To add zest to Holton's remarks, *American Rifleman* used Paul Revere and Daniel Boone as models of good Americans who knew how to defend themselves with guns. Representative Leroy Anderson (R-MT) threatened the IRS, warning it that the people held its purse strings.[23]

The NRA was successful in persuading thousands of its members to write letters to their congressmen, trumpeting the premise that legislators and law-enforcement officials wanted a police state. The organization was successful in stopping any major legislation. Congress did, however, manage to strengthen the 1938 Firearms Act somewhat. New regulations required the recording of serial numbers and retention of dealers' records for ten years instead of six, and required that serial numbers of handguns be kept permanently. But, overall, the NRA had won the gun game.

1958–1962 GUN MOVEMENT

Because the crime rate increased in the 1950s, several law-enforcement officials and congressmen continued to attempt to establish federal gun-control laws. Representative Victor Anfuso (D-NY) proposed that all privately owned pistols be registered with the FBI. The NRA responded with a flood of mail rejecting the registration of any firearm. Anfuso was the recipient of over 850 letters. A typical excerpt: "I am going to keep plenty of ammo on hand and the first son-of-a-sea-cock who tries to take my gun from me will have to shoot me first."[24]

Anfuso's bill was just one of thirty-five attempts to introduce federal gun-control legislation, and over two thousand gun bills were introduced in state legislatures. DeConde writes that the FBI estimated that crime was increasing at an annual rate of 44 percent, and the number of youth carrying guns had risen 46 percent. President Dwight D. Eisenhower—who was a strong supporter of the NRA—when asked about the public use of firearms, stated that he needed more data on the issue to fully comment on it. "But my own instant reaction," he said, "would be, well, if there weren't so many of these weapons around, why, maybe you could be a little more peaceful."[25] But Eisenhower's administration did not push for gun-control legislation.

Senator Thomas Dodd (D-CT) now chairman of the Subcommittee on Juvenile Delinquency, introduced a bill to ban the mail-order sale of pistols. The committee was successful in outlawing switchblade knives, but no gun-control legislation was passed. The NRA had won the gun game.

1963–1968 GUN MOVEMENT

After the assassination of President John F. Kennedy, the public responded by writing letters, sending telegrams, and making phone calls to their congressmen demanding immediate federal gun legislation. The NRA did not immediately react negatively to new gun-control initiatives during this period.

In 1965, Senator Dodd changed his bill (S. 214) to include the prohibition of the mail-order sale of all firearms. Dodd presented the bill to the Senate Subcommittee to Investigate Juvenile Delinquency in May 1965. The provisions of the bill were as follows:

> 1. Prohibit mail-order sales of firearms to individuals by limiting firearms shipments in interstate and foreign commerce to shipment between importer, manufacturers, and dealers.

> 2. Prohibit sales by Federally licensed importers, manufacturers, and dealers of all types of firearms to persons under 21 years of age, except that the sale of sporting rifles and shotguns could continue to be made to persons over 18 years of age.

> 3. Prohibit a Federal licensee from selling a firearm, other than a rife or shotgun, to any person who is not a resident of the State in which the licensee's place of business is located.

> 4. Curb the flow … into the United States of surplus military weapons and other firearms not suitable for sporting purposes. No one seems to know exactly how many of these surplus military weapons there are, but there must be millions of them in this country.

5. Bring under Federal control interstate shipment and disposition of large caliber weapons such as bazookas and antitank guns, and destructive devices such as grenades, bombs, missiles, and rockets.

6. Increase license fees under the Federal Firearms Acts.

7. Provide other Federal controls designed to make it feasible for States to control more effectively traffic in firearms within their borders under their police power.[26]

In order to illustrate his proposal, Dodd cited several shootings of innocent persons that had occurred in the four weeks preceding his testimony. He also cited evidence from the subpoenaed files of Klein's Sporting Goods in Chicago to prove that mail-order rifles and shotguns had been sent from that store to criminals in Chicago, Dallas, Philadelphia, Los Angeles, and the state of New York.[27]

In support of provision three (prohibiting sale of firearms to any person who was not a resident of the state) Dodd cited several cases in which persons had gone to different states to purchase guns because their own state laws had prohibited them from purchasing guns. He then asked: "How can any prudent and reasonable man maintain that we should not consider such firearms in our determination of a course of action?" Citing the records of Apple Hardware, Inc., of Chillum, Maryland, he showed that 40 percent of that company's firearm sales during 1964 and 1965 had been to residents of the District of Columbia.[28]

Dodd then turned to the provision of the bill dealing with foreign weapons. He used FBI data to show that over two million weapons had been brought into the United States from abroad during 1963 and 1964.[29] He also questioned the ethics of the opponents of gun control.

On the opening day of the hearings, Attorney General Nicholas Katzenbach addressed the subcommittee after Dodd. He also reproached the ethics of those opposed to gun-control laws. He cited, as an example, how *Shotgun News,* an NRA publication, had distorted the proposals to be discussed at those very hearings. The newspaper had reported, for example, that the sale and shipment of guns between people would give the Secretary of Treasury regulatory powers that could result in total registration. Katzenbach pointed out that the newspaper had told sportsmen: "TIME IS RUNNING OUT—OUR FRIENDS AND NEIGHBORS MUST WRITE—be courteous and brief but to the point—WRITE SOON."[30] The newspaper had reported that its goal was to have its readers write one million letters. Toward the end of his statement, Katzenbach cited J. Edgar Hoover, head of the FBI, who had said, "The spotlight of public attention should be focused on the easy accessibility of firearms and its influence on willful killing."[31]

Senator Robert F. Kennedy also addressed the hearings. He affirmed his support of Dodd's and Katzenbach's messages. Referring to the proposed bill, he said, "It would save hundreds of lives in this country and spare thousands of families all across this land the grief and heartbreak that may come from the loss of a husband, a son, a brother, or a friend.[32]

On June 8, 1965, Senator Tydings (D-MD) addressed the subcommittee. The three main points of his statement were: that nothing in the bill would prohibit the legitimate hunter from purchasing a gun; that the increased rate of crime made strict gun laws necessary; and that the NRA's legislative bulletins distorted the proposed bill. He went on: "Let me say I wholeheartedly support Senate S. 1592 and shall work for its enactment."[33]

Many speakers also spoke against Dodd's bill at these hearings. Franklin Orth, executive vice president of the NRA, defended his organization, stating that it was dedicated to national defense, law and order, and social welfare. He blamed the crime problem on the inferior economics and social status of people, on the violent crimes portrayed on the television screen, and on the pornographic emphasis of other media, such as books and magazines. He also claimed that the NRA was active in the field of firearms legislation but gave no evidence that this was the case. He felt that Senate S.1592 was a misdirected effort of "social reformers, do-gooders, or the completely uninformed who would accomplish miracles by the passage of another law." [34] Orth cited the Constitution as a precedent for not having strict gun laws. He concluded that the language of the bill was unclear, claiming that he could make no sense of it. Dodd offered to explain the parts that Orth did not understand. He then confronted Orth with the material that had been printed in *American Rifleman*, asking him to explain why the bill had been misrepresented.

On May 27, 1965, Thomas Kimball, executive director of the National Wildlife Association, presented his statement on the proposal. He said that his organization supported keeping *concealable weapons* from criminals, the mentally ill, and juveniles, and supported the prohibition of all military weapons. His basic objections were to those provisions dealing with rifles and shotguns. The main part of his speech was devoted to his own solution to the crime problem. Citing information from *U.S. News and World Report*, Kimball said: "New York City raised the strength of the police force from 244 men to 613 men for a four-month period in 1954, with all the additional policemen assigned to foot patrol.

By the end of the test period, felonies were down 55 percent, robberies were down 70 percent, burglaries were down 90 percent."[35]

Dodd concluded the hearings by stating that mail-order traffic was a means whereby criminals, addicts, and juveniles had circumvented the laws of the states and the cities of this country. He hoped that, within two weeks, action could be taken on his bill.

On July 23, 1965, there was a hearing before the House Ways and Means Committee. Chairman Wilbur D. Mills presided. Basically, the hearing was a repeat of the Senate Subcommittee to Investigate Juvenile Delinquency—Katzenbach, Orth, and Kimball all presented the same material. In addition, Leonard E. Reisman, deputy commissioner of the New York City Police Department, and J. Sills, attorney general of New Jersey, cited the high crime and murder rates in their jurisdictions as compelling reasons for federal gun legislation. Sills also criticized the tactics of the NRA, stating that pamphlets, newsletters, and *American Rifleman* had steered NRA members against gun-control laws. In his statement, Sills responded to the NRA's central arguments:

> Of course, the criminal won't register his weapon. Of course people kill people. Like the criminal who kills with an unregistered firearm. There are also unlicensed drivers who kill with automobiles. Should the conclusion then be drawn that drivers' licenses should not be required?"[36]

Sills's statement concluded with a series of rhetorical questions.

> How many more citizens will be killed in their homes, cars, or crowded places? How many more policemen will be murdered by ex-convicts who are able to purchase a firearm with no questions asked? How many more private armies will spring up and arm themselves in preparation for their self-proclaimed "day of liberty?" In fact, how many more Presidents must we lose before we come to our senses?[37]

Anti-gun-control partisans also spoke at the hearing. A typical example was Congressman John D. Dingell (D-MI), who addressed the hearing on July 22. He claimed that federal gun-control laws wouldn't eliminate the crime problem. He used the following anecdote to express his feelings:

> The Treasury Department and the Department of Justice in their pushing for their legislation are a little like a farmer that was approached by a county agent who said, "Zeke, I want to teach you how to farm with all of the newest and best methods, and I want to show you how to farm." And Zeke said, "Well

that's real good and I certainly appreciate it, but if it's all the same to you, I would just as soon not bother because I'm not farming as well as I know how right now."[38]

Although Dingell did not state his point clearly, the quote supposedly meant that law-enforcement officials were not enforcing the gun laws currently on the books. Dingell did not support Dodd's bill, as it prohibited interstate commerce in firearms and prohibited the sale of handguns outside a citizen's state of residence.

The monologues of the gun-control advocates and the NRA—and the limited dialogues between the two groups—ended without Dodd's bill being passed. At the end of 1965, therefore, the movement for gun-control laws, although it was gaining supporters, did not have the widespread support that could have brought sufficient pressure upon legislators to enact gun laws. Thus, at this time, the NRA was still winning the gun game.

During 1966 and 1967, supporters and opponents of bill S. 1592 continued to state their various viewpoints, and hundreds of articles were published attempting to explain them. President Johnson appealed to Congress's "sense of duty." He then paraphrased each provision of the revised bill:

1. Ban the interstate mail-order sale of concealable weapons.

2. Regulate the interstate sale of sporting rifles and shotguns through an affidavit provision.

3. Restrict the importation of surplus military arms and certain other foreign-made firearms.

4. Ban the sale of pistols and revolvers to persons under 21.

5. Ban the over-the-counter sale of concealable firearms to persons who are not residents of the state wherein the licensee—the dealer—does his business.[39]

The *New York Times* also reported that Dodd said: "I've never claimed that if the bill was passed it would put an end to all murders by firearms. But it would be a deterrent."[40]

The battle for gun legislation continued during 1967. In addressing the subcommittee, Orth claimed that the ideal gun legislation would provide the following types of bills:

1. A bill to provide a mandatory penalty for the use of firearms transported in interstate commerce in the commission of certain crimes.

2. A bill to provide that no licensed manufacturer or dealer may ship any firearms to any person in any state in violation of the laws of that state.

3. A bill to prohibit destructive devices (bombs, grenades, and military ordinance and similar items) under the tax and registration procedures of the National Firearms Acts.

4. A bill stipulating that a person who orders a handgun by mail or over the counter in a state other than his own must submit a sworn statement containing certain information.[41]

The provisions of Orth's proposals would not prohibit a criminal, juvenile, or mentally ill person from ordering and receiving a gun in any state except New York, New Jersey, and Missouri.

From October through December of 1967, a great deal of literature was published dealing with efforts in New York and California to pass state gun laws. Both Senator Robert Kennedy (D-NY) and Senator Edward Kennedy (D-MA) continued to push for federal gun legislation. Johnson and Dodd compromised on their proposed bill by allowing each state to decide whether to permit residents to purchase shotguns and rifles through the mail. The NRA was still winning the gun game.

In 1968, the movement for gun-control laws expanded at both the federal and state levels. On the state level, Governor George Romney (R-MI) advocated gun legislation in his state because of the Detroit riots that had occurred in 1967. Governor Nelson Rockefeller (R-NY) proposed the statewide licensing of all rifles. In Chicago, Mayor Richard Daley proposed a registration law for the city. In addition to urging the passage of state or city gun-control laws, gun-control advocates also stressed the need for uniform federal laws.

On January 3, 1968, President Lyndon B. Johnson delivered an address to Congress in which he introduced the Civil Obedience Act of 1968. The act included the following provisions:

> Whoever transports or manufactures for transportation in commerce any firearms, or incendiary device, knowing or having reason to know that the same will be used unlawfully in furtherance of civil disorder, shall be fined not more than $10,000.00, or imprisoned not more than five years, or both.[42]

On January 17, 1968, at a joint session of Congress, Johnson made reference to the above act in his "Crime Message":

> The "new law" should be coupled with Federal Firearm Bills. Both seek a common end: to reduce crime and disorder in our cities by restricting the interstate movement of two causes of death and destruction: the criminal agitator and the gun.[43]

He told Congress that its failure to act amounted to mail-order murder.

On April 4, 1968, Martin Luther King Jr. was assassinated by James Earl Ray in Memphis, Tennessee. Ray had purchased a 30.06 pump-action rifle at a Birmingham, Alabama, gun shop four days before the shooting. There had been, of course, no requirements that his fingerprints be taken or his identity established. Senator Robert F. Kennedy became the leading spokesman for gun-control laws after King's assassination. Kennedy was heckled during the Oregon primary when he spoke up for gun control. In contrast to Kennedy's support, James O. Eastland, chair of the Senate Judiciary Committee, and Richard Nixon, who was then a presidential candidate, opposed Johnson's bill, indicating it would not have prevented King's death.

On June 6, 1968, Senator Robert F. Kennedy was assassinated in Los Angeles. Legislators, the general public, and even some NRA members reacted quickly to this tragedy. As a result, there seemed to be a sense of brotherhood between pro-gun-control and anti-gun-control groups. Gimbel's Department Store, for example, appealed to the public to write their congressmen to demand immediate legislation:

> Here are the facts and questions you should ask yourself. We believe that an overwhelming majority of the people in this country want a significant gun-control law and only a small group has prevented its passage. Are you going to let this group run your life and death? Will you continue to be afraid to go out at night? The time to get action is during this session of Congress. Don't miss your chance for safety.[44]

The *New York Times* reported that many businesses, organizations, and members of the public all displayed their indignation regarding the gun problem. Some citizens turned in their guns; a Boston department store discontinued the sale of guns and ammunition at all of its branches;[45] the Southern Baptist Convention backed Johnson's bill,[46] and John Macke, the district attorney of Queens, New York, granted amnesty to anyone turning in stolen guns.[47] A spokesperson for Sears, Roebuck and Company stated that the firm would discontinue advertisements promoting firearms, ammunition, toy guns, and toys of violence.[48] A *Minneapolis Star* representative stated that the newspaper would no longer accept advertisements for rifles and shotguns.[49] Twenty-five children paraded outside a W. T. Grant's Company store in Boston, protesting the sale of toy guns.[50] Cartoons dealing with the abundance of weapons in American homes were published in the *New York Times* and stressed the point that the Second Amendment did *not* give everyone the "right to bear arms."[51] These were only a few of the events that conveyed to the nation the pressing need for gun-control laws.

The NRA did not immediately wage its typical mail campaign against gun legislation. Approximately two weeks after Robert F. Kennedy's assassination, however, the NRA convened a special conference to protest the mass attempt to disarm American citizens. Harold Glesson, the president of NRA, charged that there was a syndicated attempt to disarm American citizens by abolishing the Second Amendment. Glesson urged NRA members and affiliates to counter public pressure with a barrage of mail. He asserted that the rights of sportsmen were being threatened and revived the argument that "... registration was but the first step toward a total elimination of guns."[52] Senator Everett Dirksen (R-IL) and Senator Carl Albert (D-OK) both rejected controls over the interstate sale of rifles and shotguns.[53]

The bereaved Edward Kennedy was not active in the battle for gun-control laws during the summer of 1968. He did, however, write a letter to Dodd stating the urgent need for federal gun-control laws and asked that it be read to the Senate subcommittee at the earliest possible date. In the letter, Kennedy wrote about the power and responsibilities of Congress:

> We in Congress have it within our power now to end the interstate and mail-order gun traffic that undercuts existing State laws and provides anonymous purchasers with an easy source of implements of destruction. We have it within our power to adopt an efficient and effective national system of gun registration that will enable law enforcement authorities to tell instantaneously who is responsible for a gun used in a crime and to deter him from carrying guns in secret. We have it within our power to require that all owners and users obtain licenses so that we can screen out the criminal offenders, the addicts, the alcoholics, the juveniles, the mentally ill, and others who should not have access to guns.[54]

Historian Arthur M. Schlesinger Jr. castigated Senator Roman Hruska (R-NE) because the latter opposed Johnson's bill. Schlesinger believed that Hruska should have resigned from the Commission of Violence.[55] Postmaster General W. Martin Watson announced that no firearms sent through the mail would be delivered until local postmasters had informed law-enforcement officials of the recipient's identity.[56] Senator Mike Mansfield (D-MT) was an opponent of gun laws until Robert Kennedy's assassination. He now supported Dodd's proposal.[57] He did not, however, support Tydings's more stringent proposal to license firearm and ammunition purchasers, or the mandatory registration of all firearms.

From the middle of August until the movement's end, the amount of gun-legislation literature decreased. Nevertheless, a gun-control measure was passed in the Senate on September 17, 1968, and in the House on October 10, 1968.

The Gun Control act of 1968 …

• Prohibited convicted felons, fugitives, drug addicts, minors, mentally ill people, anyone dishonorably discharged from the military, undocumented immigrants, and people who have renounced their U.S. citizenship from buying or owning a gun.

• Required serial numbers on all guns.

• Banned mail-order sales of firearms and ammunition.

• Set minimum ages for purchases at twenty-one for handguns and eighteen for long guns.

• Banned imports of small, cheaply made handguns known as "Saturday night specials," as well as some semi-automatic assault rifles.

• Prohibited imports of foreign-made military surplus firearms.

• Required licensed dealers to keep records of firearm transactions and federal officials to inspect dealers' records of inventory.[58]

The basic purpose of the bill, as described by the Senate Judiciary Committee report, was to make it possible to keep guns from those not legally entitled to them because of age, criminal background, or mental incompetence. It was not the purpose of the act to place undue and unnecessary restrictions on law-abiding citizens. The bill was supported by President Johnson, the American Bar Association, the International Association of Police, the National Association of Citizens

Crime Commission, as well as religious and fraternal organizations. In part, gun-control advocates won this stage of the gun game.

On the surface, the bill appeared progressive, but Tydings pointed out that most individual states at the time did not have strict gun laws, which made the act less effective than it might have been. It was still possible for criminals, addicts, and juveniles to purchase guns in most states. In 1968 Tydings proposed The National Gun Crime Prevention Act (S.3634).[59] This proposed bill required every gun owner or gun purchaser to give gun information to his or her state government—or the federal government, if the state did not have licensing or registration of guns. This would provide the police with the necessary information about all guns and would, it was hoped, aid them in discovering the identity of criminals. Tydings kept fighting for common-sense gun laws. In addition, according to his bill, citizens under the age of twenty-one would not be permitted to own guns. Because the majority of senators believed that the bill was not necessary, it was defeated. Again, the NRA and pro-gun senators had won the gun game.

During the latter part of 1968, the NRA was denounced in the *Washington Post* as a "gun peddler's lobby" and as a "monstrous fraud." NRA members worked to defeat pro-gun-control candidates in the 1968 elections. DeConde writes that the more ardent gun-keepers denounced the proposed law as part of "the fetish against guns."[60] With the passing of the Gun Control Act of 1968, the movement had reached its zenith. The amount of literature soon decreased to approximately one-tenth of its level in June. Although some legislators wanted to strengthen the federal gun laws, in July of 1969, a hearing before the Senate Subcommittee to Investigate Juvenile Delinquency lasted only three days because most senators were against additional laws or modifications to the current Gun Control Act of 1968.[61]

Probably the greatest tragedies of the gun-control movement of that era were the electoral defeats of its prime advocates—Thomas J. Dodd was defeated in 1968, and Joseph Tydings was defeated in 1970.

Conclusion

This chapter has focused on the various movements for gun-control legislation from 1922 through 1968. Legislation was passed as a result of the 1934–1938 and the 1963–1968 gun movements.

The 1934–1938 gun movement occurred after the attempted assassination of Franklin D. Roosevelt. Attorney General Homer Cummings reported that 75 percent of murders were committed with concealable weapons. He believed that pistols, revolvers, machine guns, and rifles should be registered and taxed; that gun owners should be fingerprinted and photographed; and that ammunition should be regulated. Unfortunately, neither the National Firearms Act of 1934 nor the Federal Firearms Act of 1938 delivered these requirements. Many politicians, including President Roosevelt, paid lip service to federal gun laws but did not pressure Congress to pass stronger laws. The NRA magazine, *American Rifleman,* relayed bogus information to its readers that caused them to write to their congressmen demanding no strict legislation.

The reality is that if the measures proposed by Cummings had been passed, Lee Harvey Oswald probably would not have been able to purchase his mail-order rifle, and, perhaps, he would not have been able to assassinate President Kennedy. Oswald had found the advertisement for the rifle in *American Rifleman* and had used a false name to purchase the gun. The NRA did not apologize for its role in providing Oswald with the source for the gun.

If stricter federal and state gun laws existed, James Earl Ray would not have been able to purchase the 30.06 rifle he used to kill Martin Luther King.

Some mystery still exists concerning how Sirhan Sirhan obtained the pistol he used to kill Senator Kennedy. If, however, the 1934 and 1938 Firearms Acts had been passed in their original form, Robert Kennedy might not have been assassinated.

The 1963–1968 movement was more intense than the other movements. After President Kennedy was assassinated, the general public and Congress became more active in seeking federal gun legislation. On the other hand, the NRA also became more active—its membership increased by over three hundred thousand during this period. Undoubtedly, if Dr. Martin Luther King and Senator Robert Kennedy had not been assassinated, the 1968 Gun Control Bill would not have been passed.

Now, how do *you* feel about the gun movements I've described? Do you think that Attorney General Cummings was right when he stated: "Show me a man who doesn't want his gun registered, and I will show you a man who shouldn't have a gun." President Johnson said that "being allowed to purchase a gun through the mail amounts to mail-order murder." Do you agree? Franklin Orth said that those who seek gun control legislation are "social reformers, do-gooders, or the completely uninformed who would accomplish miracles by the passage of another law." Do you agree with *that*?

In this chapter, six gun movements were covered. By the close of each of these movements, the NRA, for the most part, had won the gun games. NRA executives and members are dedicated, aggressive, and determined to win every gun game they play.

At this point in the book, please reflect on the two questions posed at the beginning of Chapter 1.

> *Can we stop the cancer (proliferation of guns) from spreading, or is the gun crisis terminal?*
>
> *How can gun control advocates win the gun game?*

Key Quotation of Chapter 4

Here are the facts and questions you should ask yourself. We believe that the overwhelming majority of the people in this country want a significant gun control law and only a small group has prevented its passage. Are you going to let that group run your life and death? Will you continue to be afraid to go out at night? The time to get action is during this session of Congress. Don't miss your chance for safety.—Gimbel's Department Store

Now, please complete the Gun Movement Questionnaire: Part 1.

PART 1
GUN MOVEMENT QUESTIONNAIRE

How do you feel about the gun control efforts that took place between 1922 and 1968? Please indicate your level of agreement with the following statements.

1 = strongly disagree, 2 = disagree, 3 = undecided, 4 = agree, and 5 = strongly agree

1. _____ The sale of firearms should be carefully regulated.

2. _____ All firearms should be registered with the federal government.

3. _____ The federal government should ban the mail-order sale of firearms.

4. _____ The federal government should ban the mail-order sale of ammunition.

5. _____ The federal government should ban imports of small, cheaply made handguns known as "Saturday night specials."

6. _____ The federal government should ban imports of semi-automatic assault rifles.

7. _____ The federal government should require serial numbers on all guns.

8. _____ The federal government should require dealers to keep records of firearm transactions and authorize federal officials to inspect dealers' inventory records.

9. _____ The federal government should ban the interstate mail-order sale of concealable weapons.

10. _____ The federal government should ban the over-the-counter sale of concealable weapons.

11. _____ The federal government should ban the sale of pistols and revolvers to persons under the age of twenty-one.

12. _____ No manufacturer or dealer should be permitted to ship any firearm to any person in any state in violation of the recipient state's laws.

13. _____ Any person who orders a handgun by mail from or buys one over the counter in a state other than his own should submit a sworn statement containing certain information.

14. _____ Gun-control advocates must be misinformed do-gooders if they think that gun legislation would solve the crime problem.

15. _____ When a citizen buys a gun, he or she should be fingerprinted.

16. _____ When a citizen buys a gun, he or she should be photographed.

17. _____ Ammunition should be regulated.

18. _____ The two major causes of death and destruction are the criminal agitator and the gun.

19. _____ The greatest problem with firearms is how to keep them out of the hands of killers.

20. _____ We must not shut our eyes to the fact that there are in this country, subversive elements which desire a police state.

After you have completed the Gun Movement Questionnaire: Part 1, please read the next chapter and complete the Gun Movement Questionnaire: Part 2. After completing Part 2, review your results by going to the Meaning of Test Results section at the end of the book.

5

Gun Movements from 1986 to Today

The gun lobby in this country, though by no means certifiably psy-
chotic—their boys are smart, determined, and wealthy—does not rate
among the innocent of the world. It is demonstrably accessory to criminal
acts.[1]

—*America*

My wife, yes, my dog, maybe, MY GUN, NEVER!!![2]

—Bumper Sticker, Maryland, 1990

After Congress passed the Gun Control Act of 1968, no significant control measures left the floor of the House in the next twenty years. In the late 1960s and 1970s, a majority of NRA members were not opposed to some level of federal gun control legislation. A vocal minority, however, began a concerted effort to redefine the mission of the NRA. This effort was led by Harlon B. Carter, an executive committee member who asserted that the organization should be called the "New NRA." He criticized NRA members who believed that some gun laws were necessary for the good of society. He claimed that such thinking was "... wrongheaded and need[ed] to be replaced by the philosophy ... of absolute resistance to any and all forms of gun regulations."[3] He went on: "Any position we took [on gun control] back at that time is no good, it is not valid, and it is simply not relevant to the problems that we face today."[4] He was referring to the NRA members who supported the Gun Control Act of 1968. He even suggested that "... every gun has a legitimate purpose and ... every law-abiding person, no matter what his or her age, should have the right to choose his or her own weapon according to what he or she thinks best."[5]

The New NRA viewpoint came to dominate *American Rifleman*. Carter applied pressure to the editorial board of the magazine, stating that he "… would really raise hell with anyone who even suggested that there could be anything good about any type of gun control."[6] This led to a revolt at the NRA's annual meeting in Cincinnati in 1972. The New NRA felt that it would have more clout if it could increase its membership. Carter was able to lure new members by lowering the membership fee to fifteen dollars in the late 1970s (it was increased to thirty-five dollars in the mid-1990s). Other incentives were also available, including low-cost gun liability, theft, accidental death, dismemberment, cancer, and hospitalization insurance. Membership increased from one million in the mid-1970s to 2.6 million in 1983. By the mid-1990s, it had increased to 3.6 million.[7]

As the New NRA continued to grow and as its credibility increased, fewer gun control measures were introduced in Congress. Despite the fact that President Ronald Reagan had been a victim of gun violence, he was an enthusiastic supporter of the New NRA. When he addressed the 1983 NRA convention, he reiterated his belief that "the right of the people to keep and bear arms shall not be infringed." He concluded his speech by saying that "[W]e will never disarm any American who seeks to protect his or her family from fear or harm."[8]

Gun-control advocates, nonetheless, continued to push for stronger gun laws. From 1976 to 1980, President Jimmy Carter was a strong advocate for federal gun-control legislation, but he was unable to persuade members of Congress to pass additional legislation. He knew that the NRA had been successful in defeating Senators Dodd and Tydings, as well as over twenty congressmen in the 1970 election.

In 1974, Dr. Mark Borinsky, a victim of gun violence, created the National Council to Control Handguns (NCCH). Six years later, in 1980, it was renamed Handgun Control, Inc. (HCI). In 1983, the Center to Prevent Handgun Violence (CPHV) was established. These two organizations pushed for additional gun-control legislation.[9]

On December 8, 1980, outside the Dakota apartments in New York City, Mark David Chapman killed John Lennon with a five-shot, short-barrel, .38 caliber Charter Arms Special. Lennon's murder heightened awareness of how easy it was to buy a gun and shoot someone. According to the NRA's philosophy, Chapman, prior to killing Lennon, had been a law-abiding citizen, and, thus, should indeed have been able to purchase a gun. After he killed Lennon, he was no longer a law-abiding citizen and so should have been held responsible for his actions. Lennon's death caused HCI's membership to increase from five thousand to eighty thousand in only six weeks.[10]

On March 30, 1981, James Brady, press secretary for President Ronald Reagan, was shot in the head and injured for life. John Hinckley Jr. had used a cheap handgun to shoot Reagan, Brady and Secret Service agent Tim McCarthy. The assassination attempt caused Congress once again to reconsider federal gun legislation. The media again responded quickly by reporting on how easy it was for a formerly law-abiding citizen to obtain a handgun and use it to commit all types of crime. The assassination attempt gave credibility to the HCI argument that the United States needed stronger federal and state gun-control legislation.

The assassination attempt also persuaded Sarah Brady, James Brady's wife, to join the fight for sensible gun-control laws. She joined HCI and became its chair. In 1986, HCI successfully lobbied Congress to ban armor-piercing "cop-killer" bullets that could puncture the bulletproof vests worn by police officers. Amazingly, the New NRA was opposed to this legislation. But HCI had won this gun game.

Why would anyone be opposed to banning armor-piercing cop-killer bullets?

THE FIREARMS OWNERS PROTECTION ACT OF 1986

The Firearms Owners Protection Act of 1986 was an anti-gun-control law. Senator Robert Dole (R-KS), the Senate Majority leader, had reintroduced the bill, which had originally been known as the McClure and Volkmer bill. He believed that the bill would restrict "abuses of authority." The bill passed in the Senate by a vote of seventy-nine to fifteen. It went on to pass in the House by a vote of 292 to 130. It constituted the first comprehensive redraft of federal firearm laws since 1968. President Reagan endorsed the bill and signed it into law. He claimed that "as long as there are guns, the individual that wants a gun for a crime is going to get it."[11]

Congressmen during the Roaring Twenties had made this dubious argument when the general public clamored for gun sanity laws during that era.

The NRA spent $1.6 million to push for the passage of the bill, outspending HCI by more than six to one. Congressman Robert Torricelli (D-NJ) angrily stated that its passage was a "... genuine disgrace. It is a classic example of the power of big money and a well-orchestrated campaign by a narrow interest."[12] Wayne LaPierre, speaking for the NRA, "bragged that it had won almost everything it had sought."[13] G. Ray Arnett, executive vice-president of the NRA, predicted a rosy future for gun owners. The act removed many of the regulations established by the Gun Control Act of 1968. Specifically, it reinstated the interstate sale of rifles and shotguns and abolished the record-keeping requirements for ammunition dealers.[14] The New NRA had scored big in the gun game.

The Firearms Owners Protection Act of 1986 ...

- Allowed gun owners to transport their firearms across state lines if they were unloaded and not readily accessible.

- Made it illegal for anyone to transfer a firearm to a prohibited person.

- Limited the number of inspections on a dealer that could be made by the Bureau of Alcohol, Tobacco and Firearms without a search warrant.

- Allowed ammunition shipments through the U.S. Postal Service (a repeal of part of the GCA68).

- Prevented the government from creating a list of gun owners from dealers' records.

- Banned future sales and possession of machine guns by private citizens.[15]

THE UNDETECTABLE FIREARMS ACT OF 1988

After the passage of the Firearms Owners Protection Act of 1986, HCI focused on passing a law against undetectable guns. Two years later, in 1988, Congress passed the Undetectable Firearms Act, which banned the manufacture, importation, possession, receipt, and transfer of plastic guns capable of circumventing discovery by metal detectors. Even Ronald Reagan gave lip service to the act. Specifically, DeConde writes that Reagan had "hammered out a compromise on plastic guns that banned firearms impervious to detection by the usual security system."[16]

The HCI had won this stage of the gun game.

THE BRADY BILL

The Democratic platform for the 1992 Presidential election included "shut[ting] down the weapons bazaar," requiring a waiting period for handgun purchases, banning assault rifle weapons, enacting severe punishment for anyone selling guns to children or using a gun in the commission of a crime. When Bill Clinton became president, he also pushed for passage of an assault-weapons ban. One of his first steps was to increase the fee for a gun dealer's license from ten to two hundred dollars. This led to a decrease of more than two-thirds in the number of federally licensed dealers. In mid-February of 1993, he told Congress, "I will make you this bargain: If you will pass the Brady bill, I'll sign it."[17] In late February, Congressman Charles Schumer (D-NY) and Senator Howard Metzenbaum (D-OH) reintroduced the Brady Bill in the House and Senate. In March 1993, a Gallup poll indicated that 88 percent of the public supported the passage of the Brady Bill. The same poll reported that 77 percent—including 57 percent of gun owners—supported stricter gun laws. In September of 1993, at a public hearing, Schumer stated: "The day has passed when the NRA can bully the U. S. Congress."[18]

Several law-enforcement agencies supported the Brady Bill. These included the Fraternal Order of Police, the National Association of Police Organizations, the International Association of Black Law Enforcement Executives and the Police Executive Research Forum.[19]

Nonetheless, several congressmen spoke out against the passage of the Brady Bill. On November 10, 1993, Bill McCollum (R-FL) introduced an amendment designed to preempt all state and local waiting periods and licensing laws. This amendment was defeated. George Gekas (R-PA), however, was successful in requiring that a sunset clause be inserted to end a waiting period after five years, after which an "instant-check" computerized system would be used.[20] NRA lobbyist Wayne LaPierre characterized Clinton's efforts as "... the most intensive lobbying and arm-twisting ... ever conducted by a president of the United States on a gun-control bill."[21] But despite the anti-gun-control advocates in Congress and the gun lobby, the Brady law was passed in the Senate by a vote of sixty-three to thirty-six and in the House by a vote of 238 to 138. It went into effect on February 28, 1994.[22]

The law prohibited the following categories of persons from buying or possessing firearms:

- Those under indictment for, or convicted of, a crime punishable by imprisonment for a term exceeding one year

- Fugitives from justice

- Users of controlled substance

- Persons adjudicated as "mental defectives" or committed to mental institutions

- Illegal aliens

- Individuals dishonorably discharged from the military

- Those who have renounced their United States citizenship

- Persons subject to court order restraining a person from harassing, stalking, or threatening an intimate partner or child of the intimate partner; and those convicted of a domestic violence misdemeanor."[23]

The pro-gun control advocates had won this gun game.

Since the Brady law went into effect, more than six hundred thousand criminals have been prevented from purchasing firearms by federally licensed firearm dealers. The law, however, does not apply to unlicensed private sellers, who are not subject to background checks. Thus, there is no record of thousands of guns purchased through private sales. Despite this fact, statistics reveal significant changes between 1994 and 1998. Specifically, since 1994, the number of aggravated assaults with a firearm decreased by 31.4 percent and the number of robberies decreased by 27.8 percent. The number of murders with firearms fell by 29 percent (from 15,463 to 10,977). Overall, between 1993 and 2001, the number of gun-related deaths declined by 25 percent.[24]

Although these results were a step in the right direction, several statistics remain troubling. As reported in the Brady Campaign's *Firearms Facts,* "In 1998, 30,708 people in the United States died from firearm-related deaths—12,102 (39%) of those were murdered; 17,424 (57%) were suicides; and 866 (3%) were accidents."[25]

Here are some other troubling statistics:

- In 2001, there were approximately thirty thousand gun-related deaths in the United States—about eighty deaths per day.

- Among thirty-six high-income and upper-middle-income countries, the United States has the highest overall gun mortality rate. The rate of gun mortality in the United States is eight times higher than in other high-income countries.

- Among young people between ten and nineteen years old, there were 928 suicides with guns in 2001—more than two every day.

- The firearm death rate among children fourteen years of age and younger is nearly twelve times higher than the combined rate of twenty-five other industrialized nations.[26]

In 2000, Tom Brokaw interviewed President Clinton about the Brady law's contribution toward reducing violent crime. Clinton said: "It's given us a 35 percent drop in gun crime and a thirty-one-year low in homicide rate and kept a half million people—felons, fugitives, stalkers—from getting guns."[27] Sarah Brady, chairwoman of HCI, added: "The new FBI report demonstrates that the significant drop in the homicide rate last year is clearly linked to new efforts at gun tracing by the Bureau of Alcohol, Tobacco, and Firearms (BATF), the Brady law, and state anti-gun-trafficking initiatives."[28]

THE VIOLENT CRIME CONTROL AND LAW ENFORCEMENT ACT OF 1994

The banning of assault weapons had been talked about in Congress since the mid-1980s, but Constance Crooker writes that it was not until William Bennett, secretary of education, sent a memo to Edwin Meese, attorney general, suggesting a ban on assault weapons that action was taken in Congress.

The public expressed outrage after Patrick Edward Purdy open fired at a school playground using a Chinese version of a Soviet AK-47 in January,1989.[29] The public also expressed outrage about the increased crime rate in the late 1980s and early 1990s. As Kristine DeMay wrote at the time, "At no time since the enactment of the Bill of Rights in 1791 has the push for stricter gun control been so severe as the current push for the ban on assault rifles."[30]

Osha Davidson, in *Under Fire: The NRA and the Battle for Gun Control*, remarks that the Chinese had dumped more than eighty thousand of these weapons onto the U.S. market between 1985 and 1988, and that "people knew that these weapons were not designed to hunt squirrels."[31] Even Senator Barry Goldwater (R-AZ), a lifetime NRA member, stated that assault weapons "have no place in anybody's arsenal. If any SOB can't hit a deer with one shot, then he ought to quit shooting."[32] Likewise, President George H. W. Bush, an NRA member, on March 14, 1989, issued an executive order banning certain semi-automatic assault weapons.[33] The NRA responded by citing its traditional empty mantras: "Guns don't kill people; people kill people" and "Punish the criminal, not the tool."[34]

On August 21, 1994, forty-six Republican representatives and six senators crossed the floor and voted with the Democrats to pass the Violent Crime Control and Law Enforcement Act of 1994. It was truly a bipartisan effort, the result of six years of work. The bill was enacted on September 14, 1994. Clinton, a strong advocate for gun control, asserted that this was "the toughest, smartest crime bill in our Nation's history."[35] The bill provided for one hundred thousand new police officers, $9.7 billion in funding for prisons, and over $6 billion in funding for prevention programs.[36]

The Violent Crime Control and Law Enforcement Act of 1994 ...

- Banned the manufacture, sale and possession of nineteen types of semi-automatic assault weapons and "copycat" models, as well as other semi-automatic guns with certain characteristics.

- Outlawed magazines holding more than ten rounds of ammunition.

- Banned juvenile possession of handguns and handgun ammunition with limited exceptions, and made it a crime to sell or give a handgun to anyone eighteen or younger.

- Toughened requirements for firearms dealer licenses.

- Banned firearm possession by anyone subject to a restraining order because of threats of domestic violence.[37]

The HCI and other pro gun control advocates had scored in the gun game.

On April 27, 1999, Bill and Hillary Clinton held a press conference on gun control legislation at the White House. Hillary Clinton commented on assault weapons:

"And since the crime bill was enacted, nineteen of the deadliest assault weapons are harder to find on our streets. We will never know how many tragedies we've avoided because of these efforts."[38]

THE BRADY BILL II

After Congress passed the Violent Crime Control and Law Enforcement Act of 1994, gun-control advocates focused on further gun-control measures. Because of the successes of the Brady Bill, HCI focused on "Brady Bill II," formally titled the Handgun Control and Violence Prevention Act of 1994.

At a U.S. Senate Hearing in 1993, Senator Howard Metzenbaum (D-OH) said, "Until we can ban all of them [handguns], we might as well ban none."[39] On December 12, 1993, President Clinton ordered the Justice Department to begin studying gun licensing.[40] On February 28, 1994, Metzenbaum unveiled Brady Bill II at a press conference. The bill was designed to establish a national licensing requirement to possess a handgun and to prohibit multiple handgun purchases for transfer (handgun purchases would be limited to one per thirty-day period). The bill also mandated that all handgun dealers be strictly licensed, required that guns be registered with the BATF, and established measures to ensure that all gun dealers be of the legitimate storefront type. Gregg Carter, author of *The Gun Control Movement*, concluded that Brady II was the gun-control movement's *"pièce de résistance."*[41] He also said that the passage of Brady Bill II would be the "crowning achievement" of gun-control proponents. The bill was supported by 82 percent of adults and 72 percent of gun owners.[42]

Unfortunately, the NRA continued to fight against additional gun control measures. During the 1994 midterm election campaign, the NRA spent $70 million on political action. The NRA claimed that Democratic candidates did not keep their promises on "family values." Approximately twenty Democrats were defeated that year, including House Speaker Thomas Foley (D-WA), House Judiciary Chair Jack Brooks (D-TX), and Senate Budget Committee Chair Jim Sasser (D-TN).[43] Because of the NRA's efforts, 80 percent of its endorsed candidates won their elections. Congressman Newt Gingrich (R-GA) became the Speaker of the House. He stated that he and other gun-lobby members would work to repeal the Brady law and the limited assault-weapon ban. He also indicated that no gun-control legislation would move forward during his tenure. In addition, he created the Second Amendment Legislative Task Force "to develop a comprehensive strategy and plan that will restore rights of our citizenry to keep and bear arms ..."[44]

In 1998, Tanya Metaksa, head NRA lobbyist, summarized the NRA's strategy:

After the Brady Act and the Clinton Crime Bill became law and President Clinton proved that he would do his best to live up to our worst predictions, gun owners who didn't believe our warnings woke up. They got involved at the grassroots, and we all began to work together. The result was the 1994 elections. You remember 1994—it was payback time. United in our cause, we sent an unmistakably clear pro-Second-Amendment, pro-freedom message to the American voters and new pro-Second-Amendment congressmen to Washington. Our overwhelming success in the 1994 elections stymied Clinton's efforts to steamroller his anti-gun agenda legislatively.[45]

Overall, post-election efforts focused on the male pro-gun, pro-NRA vote which had supported conservative Republican candidates. Clinton believed that the NRA was the reason Republicans had gained control of the House.

The NRA had won this phase of the gun game.

THE ANTITERRORISM AND EFFECTIVE DEATH PENALTY ACT

During 1995 and 1996, more than two dozen gun-control bills were introduced, but none reached a vote in either House. In 1995, after Timothy McVeigh and Terry Nichols were charged in the bombing of the Alfred P. Murrah Federal Building in Oklahoma City, the media emphasized how easy it was for militia groups to purchase military-type weapons. The public was outraged at militia groups, and, as a result, both the House and Senate introduced antiterrorism bills. Even House Judiciary Chairman Henry Hyde (R-IL), who had supported a pro-gun platform in the 1980s, now became a supporter of gun control. He introduced HR 1710. This bill defined "terrorism" as the use of an explosive or firearm "other than for mere personal monetary gain [i.e., robbery], with intent to endanger, directly or indirectly, the safety of one or more individuals or to cause substantial property damage."[46]

The NRA called the bill "a loaded gun pointed at the head of the American Firearms Industry." Further, the bill made every crime committed with a gun or explosive a federal crime. The NRA fought hard against it, but the Antiterrorism and Effective Death Penalty Act passed in both houses of Congress in the spring of 1996.[47]

Gun-control advocates had won this stage of the gun game.

In 1996, Clinton was reelected. The Democratic party platform had been in favor of gun control. After the midterm elections of 1994, the NRA and pro-gun legislators had tried unsuccessfully to repeal the 1994 assault weapons ban. The NRA, however, challenged the Brady Bill in the Supreme Court in 1997. The court declared that the provision of the Brady law that required chief law enforcement to conduct background checks on prospective handgun purchasers was unconstitutional, as it infringed on the Tenth Amendment, which stipulates that the powers not delegated to the United States are reserved for the states and the people.[48]

The NRA had rebounded in the gun game.

THE DOMESTIC VIOLENCE OFFENDER GUN BAN OF 1996

Throughout the 1990s and early 2000s, women took a more active role in state elections and national elections. Mark Green, in "Voting Blocs, Building Blocks," credits women for bringing the "Gingrich revolutions to a screeching halt." He labels women as "... pink-collar female workers, the new swing voters who are concerned about wages, family leave, education, the environment, and medical care." [49] Women had expressed their concern about domestic violence. Clinton supported women on this issue, as well as regarding their concerns about public safety.

A provision of the 1994 Violent Crime Control and Law Enforcement Act had been to "Ban firearms possession by someone subject to a restraining order because of threats of domestic violence." In 1996, Senator Frank Lautenberg (D-NJ) sponsored the Domestic Violence Offender Gun Ban, which prohibited individuals with misdemeanor convictions for domestic violence from purchasing or possessing firearms.[50] Eleanor Smeal, president of the Feminist Majority Foundation, supported this gun ban, while the NRA condemned it.[51] The law was supported by the Police Foundation, the National Black Police Association, the Feminist Majority Foundation, and the National Center for Women and Policing. Research reported in the *Feminist Majority Newsletter* revealed that 40 percent of police families had experienced domestic violence. Smeal stated: "Rather than seeking exemptions for police officers who are abusers, we should be concerned with why we are recruiting so many abusers for these positions."[52]

Congress passed the bill in 1997. The law kept guns out of the hands of two thousand domestic abusers. In 1999, the Justice Department reported that more than ten thousand federal background-check applications were rejected as a result of a domestic-violence or restraining-order disqualification. During each of the following five years, approximately thirty thousand applications were rejected.[53]

The law "prohibit[ed] anyone convicted of a misdemeanor domestic violence offense from buying or owning a gun."[54]

Gun-control advocates had won this stage of the gun game.

THE FUTURE

Since 1996, only limited federal gun control has been voted out of committee; legislation has, however, passed at the state level. Congress and President George W. Bush did not push to continue the assault weapon ban, allowing it to expire in 2004. In 2005, George W. Bush and congressmen who supported the NRA—primarily Republicans—passed a bill to exempt gun manufacturers and sellers from being the targets of certain lawsuits. The results of Harris polls on gun control in 1998 and 2004 indicated that 69 percent of the general public wanted stricter federal gun laws in 1998; whereas only 52 percent of respondents wanted stricter gun laws in 2004.[55] The NRA has been successful in stopping gun legislation.

Thus, as of 2007, the New NRA is winning the gun game.

Conclusion

Between 1986 and the present, gun-control supporters have had some significant successes. These include the Undetectable Firearms Act of 1988, the Brady Bill, the Violent Crime Control and Law Enforcement Act of 1994, the Antiterrorism and Effective Death Penalty Act of 1996, and the Domestic Violence Offender Gun Control Ban of 1996.

As you were reading this chapter, were you surprised by the success of the gun-control supporters? Do you believe that these laws will help to diminish domestic violence with guns? Would you become an active member of a group that pushed for stronger federal gun-control legislation? Do you believe that NRA members are concerned about the general welfare of women and children? Why do you think that NRA members would not support legislation to ban weapons from police officers who commit domestic violence?

Key Quotation of Chapter 5

[The Brady Bill has] given us a 35 percent drop in crime and a thirty-one-year low in homicide rate and kept a half million people—felons, fugitives, stalkers—from getting guns.—President Bill Clinton

PART 2
GUN MOVEMENT QUESTIONNAIRE

How do you feel about the various gun laws discussed in the preceding chapter? Please indicate your level of agreement with the following statements.

1 = strongly disagree, 2 = disagree, 3 = undecided, 4 = agree, and 5 = strongly agree.

1. _____ Gun owners should be permitted to transport their firearms across state lines if they are unloaded and not readily accessible.

2. _____ It should be illegal to transfer firearms to a prohibited person.

3. _____ The BATF should be permitted to inspect gun dealers' records without a search warrant.

4. _____ The federal government should allow ammunition shipments through the U.S. Postal Service.

5. _____ The federal government should be permitted to create a list of gun owners from dealers' records.

6. _____ The federal government should ban the sale and possession of machine guns by private citizens.

7. The following categories of persons *should not* be allowed to purchase a firearm:

   _____ Fugitives
   _____ Users of controlled substances
   _____ The mentally ill
   _____ Individuals dishonorably discharged from the military
   _____ Those who have renounced their U.S. citizenship
   _____ Those with restraining orders against them for harassing, stalking, or threatening an intimate partner or child

8. _____ The federal government should ban the manufacture, sale, and possession of nineteen types of semi-automatic assault weapons and copycat models.

9. _____ The federal government should outlaw magazines holding more than ten rounds of ammunition.

10. _____ The federal government should ban juvenile possession of handguns.

11. _____ The federal government should ban juvenile possession of handgun ammunition.

12. _____ The federal government should toughen requirements for firearms-dealer licenses.

13. _____ The federal government should prohibit anyone convicted of a misdemeanor violence offense from buying or owning a gun.

14. _____Gun dealers who sell guns to known criminals should be held liable.

15. _____ Police officers who are convicted of domestic abuse should not be permitted to own a gun.

Now that you have completed both parts of the questionnaire, go to the Meaning of Test Results section to assess your gun-control scores.

6

Guns and Women

American Women have a superb opportunity. By reasoning with their husbands they may liberate themselves from the dark threats lurking in gun closets and bedside pistol drawers. They should do it only for their own sake. FBI reports that eight out of ten homicide victims are relatives, friends, or neighbors of the killer.[1]

—William Manchester

- How do you feel about the gun issue now?

- Have your opinions changed toward the pro-gun groups and/or the gun-control groups?

- Has your level of commitment to your opinion changed? Are you more or less polarized in your thinking?

- As you were reading the first five chapters, did you think about the relationship between guns and women?

- Have you thought about the roles women have played in the gun game?

- Have you thought about the roles women *should* play in the gun game in the twenty-first century?

As I mentioned in Chapter 1, I received over two hundred emails in response to my web-exclusive article "Ban Concealed Weapons at the U." All of the women who responded to the piece supported banning concealed weapons at the University of Minnesota.[2]

Why do you think that over 85 percent of women are in favor of strong federal gun-control laws?

71

Why do you think that only 60 percent of men are in favor of strong federal gun-control laws?

GUNS AND WOMEN: STATISTICS

The Brady Campaign's "Guns and Domestic Violence" Web site and the "Handgun-Free America—Guns and Women" Web site feature composite statistics regarding firearms and women. The following are some of the most startling of them:

- Over 50 percent of family murders are committed using firearms.

- In the United States, over 45,000 women died as a result of gun violence between 1988 and 1997. Among women twenty years of age and older, 22,614 took their own lives with guns, 21,587 were shot and killed by others, and 1,114 were killed unintentionally by firearms.[3]

- In 1997, the presence of a gun in a home made it 3.4 times more likely that a woman would become a homicide victim and 7.2 times more likely that she would be a victim of a homicide committed by a spouse or partner.[4]

- In 1998, over 3,400 women were the victims of homicide. Thirty-two percent of them (1,094) were slain by husbands or boyfriends, and 52 percent of the murders were committed with handguns.[5]

- In 1998, for every time a woman used a handgun to kill a stranger, 302 women were murdered with handguns. Women who lived in homes with guns were five times more likely to commit suicide than women who lived in homes without guns.[6]

- In 2000, firearms were responsible for the deaths of 1,120 white women, 615 African-American women, 220 Hispanic women and 104 women of other races.[7]

- In 2000, 735 women were killed by spouses or partners using guns.[8]

In addition to these startling statistics, recent research reveals that "... the female firearm homicide rate in the United States is eleven times higher than [similar rates in] all of the [other] industrialized countries combined."[9]

The NRA disputes these statistics. John R. Lott presents different data to support the NRA viewpoint. He claims that:

- When a female is confronted by a criminal, an unarmed woman is 2.5 times more likely to be seriously injured than a woman with a gun.

- According to Dr. Gary Kleck, about 205,000 women use guns every year to protect themselves against sexual abuse.

- The number of rapes in states with nondiscretionary concealed handgun laws is 25 percent lower than that in states that restrict women from carrying concealed weapons.

- Over 500 women use firearms to defend themselves against sexual assault or abuse each day—that is 20 defenses an hour or 1 every 3 minutes. [10]

As you can see, the statistical data is quite different between the pro-gun group and the gun-control group. Which side is telling the truth? According to the Bureau of Statistics, over two thousand women were killed by firearms in 2000. Do you believe the results reported by the Bureau of Statistics? Do you believe the NRA statistics that claim that over five hundred women defend themselves against sexual assault every day? This would mean that there are over 182,500 attempted sexual assaults of women in the United States each year. The NRA's statistics did not come from the Bureau of Statistics. John Lott uses a statistical model to project the number of attempted rapes. Do you believe *real* data or *projected* data? Do you question the accuracy of the NRA's data?

NRA MYTHS

Between 6 and 10 percent of American women own guns. The NRA has generated four myths about guns and women.

Myth: Guns protect women from gun violence.

Fact: Rates of female homicide, suicide, and unintentional firearm death are disproportionately higher in states where guns are more prevalent.[11]
Fact: In the United States, regions with higher levels of handgun ownership have higher suicide rates.

Myth: Handgun ownership increases women's ability to defend themselves.

Fact: Women are 101 times more likely to be murdered with a handgun than to use a handgun to kill in self-defense. Women also were eighty-three times more likely to be murdered by a husband or partner with a handgun than to kill their partners.[12]

Myth: Guns protect women against rape.

Fact: Less than 2 percent of rapes are committed by men with guns. Thus, women would be safer using self-defense tactics to fight off attackers.[13]

Myth: Women need guns to protect against stranger rape.

Fact: Only 25 percent of rapes are committed by strangers. [14]

WOMEN'S ORGANIZATIONS FOR GUN CONTROL

The Brady Campaign to Prevent Gun Violence (BCPGV)

This organization is led by Sarah Brady. She joined the organization after her husband James Brady, Ronald Reagan's press secretary, was shot in the head. The organization's Web site cites facts, briefs, research, and statistics regarding a variety of gun issues. The site's section on legislation enables readers to monitor their elected officials' voting records on gun control. The Brady Center provides timely and valuable information on gun violence. The center's programs include A Day in the Neighborhood, Clarence's Adventures, and the Hechinger Speakers Bureau. It also publishes fact sheets on the latest gun violence statistics, works with Law Enforcement Relations, The Legal Action Project and Steps to Prevent Firearm Injury in the Home.

The BCPGV also files suits against gun dealers for straw sales of guns, files suits against gun sellers who supplied trafficking rings with hundreds of guns, conducts fundraising events across the country, and files suits against gun dealers with long criminal records. The BCPGV supports police officers who want to bring suits against negligent gun sellers.[15]

The Children's Defense Fund Gun Violence Program (CDFGVP)

The CDFGVP's mission is to "leave no child behind" and to ensure every child a "Healthy Start, a Fair Start, a Safe Start, [and] a Moral Start" in life and a successful passage to adulthood. This nonprofit organization is supported by corporate grants and individual donations, and it is not supported by the federal government.

The organization maintains statistical records and fact sheets regarding children and gun violence, the basics of gun-safety legislation, community action toolkits, annual data reports, and articles on the early recruitment of children into the gun culture.[16]

The Million Mom March (MMM)

The MMM's Web site claims that it is the "nation's largest grassroots, non-partisan, chapter-based organization" involved in the fight to prevent gun violence. The MMM has united with the BCPGV in an attempt to create an America free from "gun violence, where all Americans are safe at school, at work, and in their communities."[17]

The original Million Mom March, a public anti-gun demonstration, was held in Washington, D.C., on Mother's Day, May 15, 2000. Approximately 750,000 people took part. Many impassioned women speakers spoke about the tragedy of gun violence in the United States by sharing stories about their own children who died of gun wounds. Donna Dees-Thomases, the march's primary planner, had been inspired to organize the march after watching a news report describing a shooting at a Jewish community center in Los Angeles. She had been shaken and outraged by TV images of preschoolers being forced out of a day camp after a gunman went on a rampage. In addressing the MMM audience, she said: "Twenty-five years ago, Barry Goldwater said he was opposed to gun control because there were so many guns in this country that it would take fifty years to get them at a reasonable level. Well, had we done it twenty-five years ago, we'd be halfway there."[18] Other speakers included Sarah Brady, Representative Carolyn McCarthy, Hillary Clinton, and President Bill Clinton. Many celebrities also spoke at the event.[19]

As I mentioned in Chapter 1, this event was one of the reasons that prompted me to write this book. I watched the event on C-SPAN for several hours, and I felt emotionally drained after listening to so many tragic stories of gun violence.

Some demonstrators—primarily women—pushed strollers holding children while others carried signs with slogans such as "Melt the Guns" and "Be Mad about Guns." President Clinton received the "Mom's Apple Pie Award" for his continuing support for more federal gun legislation.[20]

The MMM organization had asked its members to send emails to their congressional representatives urging them not to take away the rights of gun-violence victims. For the previous seven years, members of the NRA had been emailing their representatives demanding that gun dealers be exempt from lawsuits initiated by innocent victims. The MMM has asserted:

> Remember the NRA and the gun corporations are pushing this legislation because we are beating them and they are scared that the average citizen will hold them accountable for their reckless actions. Together we can make a difference—we can beat this legislation and stop the NRA in its tracks.[21]

Unfortunately, the NRA had more legislative support on the issue. Thus, it had won that particular gun game.

The MMM organization "... issues briefs and an explanation of gun laws state-by-state, provides legislative updates to local chapter founders, presents Apple Pie Awards to notable people who campaign for stronger gun-control laws, and time-out chairs for people who support the gun lobby." The MMM has urged members to do the following:

JOIN US!

Step One: Contact Congress

Contact your Representative and give him/her a simple message: Oppose HR 800—a bill that would deprive gun-violence victims of their legal rights. Reckless gun-sellers should not get special legal privileges.

Step Two: Add Your Name to the List

Individuals: Sign the Petition
Organizations: Download the Endorsement Form

Step Three: Tell Others

Help us grow our grassroots coalition by sending an e-mail to your friends, family, and co-workers about the Campaign.[22]

Mothers Against Teen Violence (MATV)

MATV was born after the tragic death of Charles Christopher Lott on June 19, 1993, in Dallas, Texas. Chris and his friend, Kendrick, had been "accosted by two delinquent teens that were armed with handguns and under the influence of alcohol and illegal drugs."[23] They were killed with 9 mm handguns.

From 1993 to 2000, MATV was a community-based organization that offered both violence-prevention and victim services. In 2000, MATV became a national organization. Its primary purpose is to make schools and communities safer through teen violence prevention. MATV's Web site provides advice for parents to deal with their children's behavior and provides statistics on children and gun violence. The Web site claims that there are enough guns in America to provide every adult citizen with one. Of the approximately 220 million firearms in the United States, 67 million are handguns. The MATV mission is "to make schools and communities safer through effective teen violence prevention."[24]

Mothers Against Violence in America (MAVIA)

MAVIA, founded in 1994, is a leader in the field of violence prevention. It has created strong partnerships with schools, businesses, and community leaders throughout the United States. It presents several ways to reduce violence. These include rejecting violence as a means of solving problems or disputes, standing up against bigoted behavior, networking with other parents to know where your children are and whom they are with, supporting legislation that addresses both the causes of and factors that magnify violence, and volunteering to mentor children in the juvenile justice system. It also advises, "If there are children in your home, the decision to own a gun should be considered very seriously. If you choose to own a gun, make sure it is stored in a locked, secure place where children cannot gain access to it."[25]

The MAVIA Web site suggests:

1. Letting your children see you stand up peacefully against bigoted behavior or comments.

2. Getting to know your children.

3. Becoming a member of MAVIA and help to fortify a national network of mothers, fathers, students, and others committed to putting a stop to violence by and against children.

Deborah Prothrow-Stith, MD, assistant dean of the Harvard School of Public Health's Government and Community Programs, states, "I have a deep appreciation for MAVIA in that it provides survivors of violent crimes with a platform to tell their stories and have an impact on violence prevention."[26]

This organization's Web site includes ways to take action and presents video and Web resources and links to related topics. MAVIA's mission is "Preventing violence by and against children through education, outreach, and advocacy."[27]

WOMEN'S ORGANIZATIONS OPPOSED TO GUN CONTROL

Armed Females of America (AFA)

The AFA's mission is to "proudly represent all patriotic, strong, intelligent people who believe that 'no-compromise means our rights and liberties aren't bargained for ...'" The AFA describes its members as "freedom-loving Americans," and claims that "our right to keep and bear arms is an individual, inalienable right endowed by our creator, guaranteed by the Second Amendment of the Bill of Rights, and directly supports our lives, liberties, safeties, and pursuits of happiness."[28] AFA members also believe that the Second Amendment is a God-given right that cannot be legislated against.

It is hard to believe, but AFA also claims that any law restricting gun use, quantity of guns owned or purchased, magazine capacity, configuration, caliber, firing operation, or age limitation is unconstitutional. Their philosophy appears to be that anyone should be able to purchase any gun at any age. The AFA asserts that gun control has been a "colossal failure" and a national embarrassment. Its mission statement concludes: "WITH GOD'S BLESSING and our diligence, we aim to remain FREE!"[29]

The AFA's Web site also contains updates on current events and opinion pieces, a section of notable quotations, gun safety tips, and extensive links to the Web sites of other gun-rights organizations.

Mothers Arms (MA)

MA is a national nonprofit organization "created to inform, educate, and support the development of self-reliant women nationwide." Its mission statement says that "Women and children may now face crazed gunmen and terrorists while in school, home, play, or their place of worship."[30] Members must protect their children, they claim, by teaching them how to protect themselves.

Alicia Wadas, founder and president of MA, suggests that visitors read its newsletter, which provides common-sense tips and techniques for protecting oneself. Wadas has attended firearm-education classes and has taught her children gun safety. As president of MA, she teaches family-safety plans and defense tools. The organization says that it is concerned about the safety of mothers and their children. Its motto is "Our Children, Our Family, Ourselves."[31]

National Rifle Association Women (NRAW)

NRAW was created to provide a wide range of programs for women from all walks of life. It has programs for women on hunting, shooting, and crime prevention. It also invites women to become political activists. NRAW claims that two million American women hunt and that an additional four million enjoy target-shooting. NRAW teaches firearm-safety strategies; presents information on women's special events at NRA annual meetings; publishes a newsletter, hunting articles, and safety and training resources; and runs the "Eddie Eagle Gun Safe Program," which seeks to prevent the involvement of young children in gun accidents.

The National Rifle Association has created a new official journal called *Women's Outlook*. Like the NRA's other journals, *Women's Outlook* focuses on perceived Second-Amendment rights. It includes editorials, commentaries, and feature articles. Its motto is: "Refuse to Be a Victim."[32]

Second Amendment Sisters, Inc. (SAS)

SAS is based in Lakeway, Texas. Its Web site includes a self-defense section, newsletters archive, articles including safety tips and gun facts, a press area with rally reports, a talk-back section, suggested readings, and educational links about firearm safety. Its motto is "Self-Defense is a Basic Human Right."[33] The organization's Second Amendment Foundation publishes *Women and Guns Magazine*, in which women have an opportunity to publish editorials and state viewpoints on gun rights.

Women Against Gun Control (WAGC)

WAGC states: "Women are concerned about becoming victims of crime. Guns give women a fighting chance against crime." WAGC advocates the gun as the great equalizer in women's self-defense. Its Web site says that gun control is:

> The theory that a woman found dead in an alley, raped and strangled with her panty hose, is somehow morally superior to a woman explaining to police how her attacker got that fatal bullet wound.

It also cites Susan B Anthony: "A woman must not depend upon the protection of a man, but must be taught to protect herself." It concludes: "Visit our web page often for the 'Ammunition' you need to 'arm yourself' against gun control."[34]

WAGC's seems to be the most sophisticated of the anti-gun-control Web sites directed at women. It even includes a "pledge:"

WOMEN AGAINST GUN CONTROL PLEDGE

You qualify to be a member of WAGC if:

1. You vote.

2. You believe in and work to preserve the Second Amendment.

3. You exercise safety and responsibility in handling of firearms.

4. You don't believe that guns cause crime.

5. You promise to never cause bodily harm to anyone unless acting in self-defense.

Its motto is: "Guns SAVE LIVES. We do NOT support gun control. Gun Control does NOT control crime."[35]

COMPARING GROUPS FOR AND AGAINST GUN CONTROL

Now that you have had an opportunity to read about women's organizations for gun control and against it, how would you evaluate each group? Both sides have deep-seated feelings about the gun issue, and women on both sides of the issue seem to be people of goodwill.

How would you rate the pro-gun-control groups? The BCPGV and MMM are the largest such organizations and seem to appeal to a more diverse audience. The BCPGV introduced the Brady Bill and played significant roles in the passage of the Violent Crime Control and Law Enforcement Act of 1994 and the Domestic Violence Offender Gun Ban of 1996. The MMM organization is directly linked to the BCPGV. Together, they were successful in persuading Congress to pass gun-control legislation that made our country safer. More specifically, they created a safer environment for women. It is hard to believe that any women's organizations would be opposed to these bills.

> *Why would anyone be opposed to banning gun possession by individuals convicted of domestic violence? How can such a stance possibly be justified?*

The BCPGV and MMM mission is to "create an America free from gun violence, where all Americans are safe at school, at work, and in their communities." The CDFGVP, MATV, and MAIVA are concerned primarily with children. The CDFGVP's mission is to "leave no child behind," MATV's is to "make schools and communities safer through effective teen violence prevention," and MAVIA's is to "prevent violence by and against children through education, outreach, and advocacy."

These five organizations support gun-control laws. They believe that federal gun-control legislation will help to decrease the number of murders of women and children and that education and parent involvement will decrease the crime rate. Members of these organizations support a nonviolent approach in the gun game.

How do you rate the pro-gun groups? The AFA describes its members as "freedom-loving Americans" who believe strongly in their interpretation of the Second Amendment. The AFA believes that law-abiding citizens have a "God-given right" to purchase any type of firearm. The NRAW group is part of the NRA and "promotes hunting, shooting, and crime prevention." In its journal, *Women's Outlook*, members publish editorials, commentaries, and articles. It is politically active and pushes the NRA agenda. Its motto insists that "members refuse to be victims."

SAS also supports the NRA's objectives. Its motto is "Self-defense is a basic human right." The SAS seems to believe that if a person promotes federal gun-control legislation, that person is not interested in the welfare of women. WAGC members believe that guns give women a fighting chance against rape and other crimes. The MA organization believes that mothers need to teach their children how to protect themselves—that children need to be educated about guns and gun safety. MA's motto is "Our Children, Our Family, Ourselves."

These organizations all believe that the Second Amendment guarantees all law-abiding citizens a right to bear arms—which they interpret to include all types of firearms. Women opposed to gun control do not promote violence but promote self-defense by using firearms. They also support the NRA agenda.

Conclusion

Now that we've discussed guns and women, do you agree with the pro-gun-control groups or the pro-gun groups on the subject? Should representatives from each of these groups conduct a dialogue to determine areas of agreement and disagreement? If you are a woman, would you like to participate in such a discussion of the gun-control issue? If you are a man, would you like to discuss the gun control issue with women? At this time, do you think we need to have additional federal gun legislation to protect women?

Key Quotation from Chapter 6

Remember the NRA and the gun corporations are pushing this legislation (urging Congress to take away the right of gun violence victims) because we are beating them and they are scared that the average citizen will hold them accountable for their reckless actions. Together we can make a difference—we can beat this legislation and stop the NRA in its tracks.–MMM

Websites of Women's Organizations in favor of Gun Control

The Brady Campaign to Prevent Gun Violence
www.bradycampaign.org

Children's Defense Fund Gun Violence Program
www.childrendefense.org

Million Mom March
www.millionmommarch.org

Mothers against Teen Violence
www.matvinc.org

Mothers against Violence in America
www.ci.tukwila.wa.us

Websites for Women's Organizations Opposed to Gun Control

Armed Females of America
www.armedfemalesofAmerica.com

Mothers Arms
www.mothersarms.org

National Rifle Association Women
www.nrahq.org

Second Amendment Sisters, Inc.
www.2sisters.org

Women against Gun Control
www.wagc.com

Now, please indicate your level of agreement with the following Guns and Women Questionnaire.

GUNS AND WOMEN QUESTIONNAIRE

Please indicate your level of agreement with each of the following statements.

1 = strongly disagree, 2 = disagree, 3 = undecided, 4 = agree, and 5 = strongly agree.

1. _____ Owning a gun will protect women from violent crime.

2. _____ I would join women's groups opposed to gun control.

3. _____ Guns protect women from rape.

4. _____ Guns save lives.

5. _____ The Brady Campaign to Prevent Gun Violence should file lawsuits against gun dealers for straw sales of guns.

6. _____ Women would be safer using self-defense tactics to fight off attackers rather than using guns.

7. _____ The Second Amendment is a God-given right.

8. _____ Gun control does not control crime against women.

9. _____ I believe that using guns for self-defense is a basic human right.

10. _____ I would join women's gun-control groups.

11. _____ I would carry a sign stating "Be Mad about Guns" at a rally.

12. _____ I would/will teach my child[ren] to reject gun violence as a means of solving problems.

13. _____ Handgun ownership increases women's ability to defend themselves.

14. _____ The Million Mom March organization is concerned about gun-violence victims.

15. _____ Women need guns to project themselves against stranger rape.

16. _____ I believe that women should try to make schools and communities safer through effective teen violence protection.

17. _____ I believe that mothers can prevent violence through education, outreach, and advocacy.

18. _____ Guns give women a fighting chance against crime.

19. _____ I believe that the Million Mom March should occur annually.

20. _____ Gun control groups promote a nonviolent approach to the gun game.

Please review your results by going to the Meaning of Test Results section.

7

Guns and Children

American children are more at risk from firearms than the children of any other industrialized nation. In one year, firearms killed no children in Japan, nineteen in Great Britain, fifty-seven in Germany, 109 in France, 153 in Canada and 5,285 in the United States.[1]

—Centers for Disease Control, 1997

Children with guns don't kill people; children with no moral values kill people.[2]

—www.jeremiahproject.com

Guns that cannot be locked away should be stored unloaded with a trigger lock in place.[3]

—www.jcfcc.vcn.com

This chapter focuses on guns and children. I imagine that some of you were exposed to shotguns, rifles, and handguns as you were growing up. As I reflect on this topic, I can clearly remember where my father kept each of his guns. His two unloaded shotguns were braced against the wall in the dining room, by the refrigerator. The rifles were kept in his bedroom closet upstairs, which my brother and I were told never to enter. There was no lock on the closet door. The ammunition was kept on the top shelf of the closet in the stairway. A stepladder was necessary in order to get the ammunition down. My father told my brother and me that only he could retrieve the ammunition. When I was twelve, however, I used a rake to get the shotgun shells down. I had been careful not to remove the rifle shells. As I reflect on the situation, I realize that I should have been punished, even though my actions had no negative consequences.

As we begin this chapter, think about your childhood experiences with guns.

- Did your parents or guardians own guns?

- Did you have access to the guns?

- Did your parents teach you about the proper use of firearms?

- Did you take a gun-safety course?

- How did you feel about having guns in the house?

- Did you ever use a gun without a parent's permission?

- Do you believe that all guns should be kept in a secure place where children do not have access to them?

- Do you believe that all guns should have trigger locks?

- Do you believe that, if parents are careless with guns and a child is injured or killed, the parents should be held legally responsible for the injury or death?

- If a child uses a gun to commit a crime, should the parents be held legally responsible for the crime?

STARTLING FACTS ABOUT GUNS AND CHILDREN

- Of the 3,012 U.S. children and teens killed by gunfire in 2000 …

  1,776 were murdered by gunfire

  1,007 committed suicide with a firearm

  193 died as a result of accidental shootings

  1,762 were white

  1,149 were black

  568 were Hispanic

  433 were under age fifteen

  129 were under age ten

  59 were under age five[4]

- 80 percent of murder victims aged thirteen to nineteen were killed with fire-arms.[5]

- The rate of firearm deaths of under-fourteen-year-olds is nearly twelve times higher in the United States than in twenty-five other industrialized countries combined.

- In a study of inner-city seven-year-olds and their exposure to violence, 75 percent reported having heard gunshots.[6]

- The firearm-injury epidemic—due largely to handgun injuries—is ten times larger than the polio epidemic of the first half of the twentieth century.[7]

- Between 1979 and 2000, nearly 90,000 children and teens were killed by gunfire; 61 percent were white, and 36 percent were black.

- According to the Children's Defense Fund, in 1999, 3,365 children and teens were killed by gunfire.

  1,990 of them were murdered.

  1,078 committed suicide.

  214 died of accidental shooting.[8]

- The gun industry is exempt from federal health and safety requirements, such as one that would mandate internal trigger locks. Toy guns and teddy bears are subject to higher consumer health and safety standards.[9]

- According to the Centers for Disease Control and Prevention, every seven hours a teen dies from a firearm accident or by suicide.

- The United States has the highest rates of childhood homicide, suicide, and firearm deaths among all of the industrialized countries.

- The homicide rate for U.S. children is five times higher than for children in twenty-five other industrialized countries combined.[10]

- Gun killings by young people between the ages of eighteen and twenty-four increased from about 5,000 to about 7,500 between 1980 and 1997.[11]

- Almost 80 percent of Americans think that it is important to reduce children's access to guns.[12]

SCHOOL SHOOTINGS

"A Time Line of Recent Worldwide School Shootings," lists thirty-nine school shootings in chronological order between February 2, 1996 and March 21, 2005. Thirty of the thirty-nine school shootings—more than 75 percent—occurred in the United States. The following are summaries of some of the U.S. shootings:

- Two students and one teacher killed, one other wounded when a fourteen-year-old opened fire on his algebra class on February 2, 1996, in Moses Lake, Washington.

- Three students killed and five wounded by a fourteen-year-old boy as they participated in a prayer circle at Heath High School on December 1, 1997, in Stamps, Kentucky.

- One teacher killed, two students wounded at a dance at James W. Parker Middle School on May 19, 1998, in Edinboro, Pennsylvania.

- Fourteen students (including killers) and one teacher killed, twenty-three others wounded at Columbine High School on April 20, 1999, in Littleton, Colorado.

- One student killed at Lake Clifton Eastern High School on January 17, 2001, in Baltimore, Maryland.

- Two students killed and thirteen wounded by a fifteen-year-old boy firing from a bathroom at Santana High School on March 5, 2001, in Santee, California.

- One teacher, a security guard, five students, the shooter's grandfather, the grandfather's companion, and the shooter himself killed on March 21, 2005, in Red Lake, Minnesota.[13]

An examination of the list reveals that in ten of the thirty cases, the shooters were fourteen or younger. They were all males. The killings occurred throughout the United States; the killings occurred primarily in small towns; the killings did not appear to be drug-related. Most of the weapons used belonged to family members. Although rifles and shotguns were used in some killings, the primary weapons were handguns.

WHERE JUVENILES OBTAIN GUNS

In 1993 and 1994, the Bureau of Alcohol, Tobacco, and Firearms (BATF) conducted tracing programs to discover the sources of firearms recovered from juvenile offenders. It conducted more than 3,800 traces. The results revealed that 27 percent of offenders had been given firearms by sources other than their parents or guardians, while 22 percent had obtained firearms in burglaries and other thefts. The investigators also discovered that 16 percent had purchased their firearms on the street, and 15 percent had taken firearms from their homes. The BATF could not trace the sources of 20 percent of the weapons.[14]

PRO-GUN-CONTROL ORGANIZATIONS FOR CHILD SAFETY

The American Academy of Child and Adolescent Psychiatry (AACAP)

The AACAP is a "national, professional, non-profit medical organization established in 1953 to support and advance child and adolescent psychiatry." The organization asserts: "We cannot gun-proof our children and adolescents." It understands that it is common sense that children are playful and active. Likewise, teenagers are curious and impulsive. These are natural traits that, when mixed with guns, can cause or lead to death.

The AACAP states that, "The best way to protect children against gun violence is to remove all guns from the home." If, however, firearms *are* kept in the home, the gun owner should:

• Store all firearms unloaded and uncocked in a securely locked container. Only the parent should know where the container is located.

• Store the guns and ammunition in separate, locked locations.

• For a revolver, place a padlock around the top strap of the weapon to prevent the cylinder from closing, or use a trigger lock for a pistol.

• When handling or cleaning a gun, never leave it unattended—even for a moment; it should be in your view at all times.[15]

Parents should also be aware that children with emotional problems are more likely to use guns against themselves and others. If necessary, parents should have their children evaluated by a psychiatrist or other qualified mental-health professional.

The National Association of School Psychologists (NASP)

The NASP's mission is to be "effective partners in commitment to help school children and youth achieve their best. In school. At home. In life." The organization believes that the increasing presence of guns in society may create a threatening and hostile climate that could adversely affect children's psychological development and learning.

The Executive Board of NASP resolves to:

1. Support public polices on gun control which effectively address the potential physical and psychological harm that guns may cause children;

2. Promote the development of policies and practices within schools and communities which effectively address potential physical and psychological harm that guns and other weapons might cause for children;

3. Assist policy makers, community leaders, parents, educators, school psychologists, and others with creating safe environments for children and protecting the physical and psychological well-being of children; and

4. Work collaboratively with other professional and advocacy groups in the implementation of the practices described in this resolution.[16]

The American Academy of Pediatrics (AAP)

The AAP is "dedicated to the health and well-being of infants, children, adolescents, and young adults." The organization believes that, as educators of children, parents play a primary role in preventing gun violence. It suggests four steps to follow to reduce gun violence:

1. The single most important step is to keep guns away from children.

2. Make sure that your children know the dangers of guns and not to touch and handle guns.

3. Talk to your children about guns and violence.

4. Talk to your children about the differences between media violence and violence in the real world.[17]

Safer Child, Inc. (SCI)

SCI's mission is to help "make the world a healthier and safer place for children." The group suggests that banning guns won't guarantee safety, but it says that "Guns are not cool. They are not fun ... you must make sure that your child knows exactly what to do when confronted with a situation."[18]

Here are SCI's "Basic Tips for firearm Safety:"

• Always lock your firearms when they are not being used.

• Always assume that your firearm is loaded—and handle it in that way.

• Use a good locking device.

• Never ever point a firearm at anyone in fun.

• Teach your children that if they see a gun, they should not touch it, and should immediately leave the area to go tell an adult.

• Do not assume that other adults think the same way you do.

On August 20, 2001, SCI and the AAP held their first "National Ask Day," on which parents were encouraged to ask neighbors about guns in their homes before allowing their children to play there.[19]

Women Against Gun Violence (WAGV)

WAGV began in 1993. Los Angles Police Commissioner Ann Reiss Lane coordinated the program. The coalition's purpose is to change the "climate of the gun-violence debate by working with elected officials, survivors, and communities."

Here are WAGV's guiding principles:

- We have the right to be free from gun violence in our homes, streets, schools, places of work, and communities.

- The presence and availability of firearms pose a significant threat to the safety of our communities.

- Gun violence is a critical public health, safety, social, and economic issue costing thousands of lives and billions of dollars every year.

- To prevent gun violence, access to and availability of handguns, assault weapons and ammunition must be reduced.

- Safety mechanisms must be maximized on guns that are produced and sold and consumer product safety laws must apply equally to firearms.[20]

WAGV believes that gun manufacturers and lobbyists have targeted women in order to exploit their fears of crime and violence. Women, however, should know that guns should be feared more than intruders and that a gun in the home increases the danger to women and children. WAGV reports several important facts. Among them: more teenagers are killed in the United States with guns than in any other country; every six hours, a young person uses a gun to commit suicide; and having a gun in the home makes it three times more likely that a family member will be killed by a gun.[21]

A major focus of WAGV is to provide information to parents about the dangers of guns in the home. The organization suggests that parents should make sure that their children understand that "guns are real and kill people." WAGV provides separate guidelines for talking with children aged three to eight and eight to ten. The organization stresses listening to your children and explaining to them the consequences of being around guns.[22]

CHILD ACCESS PREVENTION (CAP) LAWS

All pro-gun-control organizations support CAP laws. These laws, often referred to as "safe storage" or "gun owner responsibility" laws, require the owners of guns to store them in places that are inaccessible to children or to use devices to lock the guns. James and Sarah Brady state that CAP laws are necessary to prevent accidental shootings, suicides, and murders. Nineteen states have laws or legal holdings that specifically hold gun owners responsible for leaving firearms where they are easily accessible to children.[23]

CAP laws are important when you consider that, in 2000, an American youth committed suicide with a firearm every eight hours [24] and an American youth was murdered with a firearm every four and a half hours.[25]

The NRA criticizes these laws, and its members raise certain questions:

Do CAP laws work, or are they 'feel-good' laws?

Answer: CAP laws work. CAP laws raise public awareness of the primary problems and provide simple solutions.

Will grief-stricken parents be imprisoned for the death of their children?

Answer: Not necessarily. The laws' purpose is to deter negligent gun storage in order to protect children.

Does the use of an effective child-safety lock impair the ability to use a gun for self-defense?

Answer: No.

Do CAP laws prevent children from hunting and fishing?

Answer: No. The laws are concerned with safe storage of loaded guns.[26]

OTHER VIEWPOINTS ON GUNS AND CHILDREN

The Jeremiah Project (JP)

Unlike the previously mentioned organizations, which focused on gun safety, the Jeremiah Project identifies sources of the gun-violence problem. JP specifically blames divorce for the increase in children's access to guns. Members of the organization believe that children and adolescents have abandoned the traditional notions of *right* and *wrong* and personal responsibility. It does not, however, discuss how young people should go about obtaining these notions. JP also believes that gun violence is a result of God being banned from our schools.

Despite research that concludes poverty drives children to violence, JP dismisses violence and poverty as reasons why children turn to guns. In addition, JP asserts that liberals ignore the personal responsibility of each and every one of us. It castigates liberals for their permissive attitudes, but it does not provide support for its claim that these attitudes are detrimental. I myself am a liberal, and I believe that both conservatives and liberals are fully capable of personal responsibility.

JP also contends that our schools are teaching children that premarital sex is all right if they practice safe sex and protect themselves from disease. Perhaps, JP can provide a list of schools that teach these practices. JP claims that a government that lives off of "society's moral decay" is another reason for the out-of-control violence in our society

The group's Web site introduces Darrell Scott, who is the father of two Columbine High School shooting victims. We are provided with an account of the address he made to the House Judiciary Committee's Subcommittee on Crime on May 27, 1999. He spoke about good and evil, after which he delivered a poem accusing legislators of having ignored the deepest needs of children by outlawing prayer in public schools. The poem concluded: "You regulate restrictive laws/ Through legislative creed/And yet you fail to understand/That God is what we need!"

It was a very moving poem, and Mr. Scott might even be correct about our society, but the absence of religiosity in public schools does not account for how Eric Harris and Dylan Klebold obtained their firearms, killed twelve innocent people, and injured twenty-three others.[27]

The NRA's Determination

The gun lobby and gun industry claim that they have found the solution to the problem of guns and children: "What the kids need are more guns." The NRA asserts that kids need an early familiarity with firearms, culminating in ownership, as this is the foundation of patriotism and civil virtue.[28]

In the March 2000 issue of *American Guardian* magazine, Wayne LaPierre, the executive vice-president of the NRA, said that the fight was about protecting children from an America dominated by pro-gun-control media and politicians.[29]

NRA executives acknowledge that they have lost much of a generation of youth to video games and a general decline in interest in shooting sports. Marion Hammer, the NRA's first woman president, said: "I know that when the NRA reaches out and takes the hand of a child, we are touching America's future." She continued by stating that the NRA needs to build a bridge to the American youth and to teach children the value of gun rights. She went on: "If we do not successfully reach out to the next generation, then the freedom and liberty that we've lived for—and that many of our ancestors have died for—will not live beyond us."[30]

The NRA is fighting for its survival. A 1998 poll, for example, claims that only 15 percent of American youth owned their own guns.[31]

The National Shooting Sports Foundation (NSSF) claims that its purpose is to "... provide trusting leadership in addressing industry challenges and in delivering programs and services to meet the identified needs of our members."[32] Josh Sugarmann writes that a 1994 NSSF brochure, "When Your Youngster Wants a Gun," asked the question, "How old is old enough?" the response indicates that maturity and individual responsibility, rather than age, should provide the answer. Some might be ready at ten, while others may not be ready until fourteen. That is, if a youngster follows directions well, is conscientious, reliable, and responsible enough to be home on his own for two or three hours or sent to a grocery store with a list and twenty dollars, he is responsible enough to have his first gun.[33] If this logic holds, some people might never be mature enough to own guns, no matter how old they are, and these are the ones from whom gun-control laws seek to protect the general public.

The NSSF brochure encourages parents to introduce firearms to children as young as four or five.

Since hunting has declined and there is currently no universal military service—two traditional ways in which children were introduced to guns—the gun industry has become more creative in enticing children to become involved in shooting. It has turned to "combat shooting." Sugarmann says that this is

> ... a run-and-gun, shoot-to-kill activity in which participants use pistols, assault rifles, and combat shotguns in "real-life" situations against humanoid targets—to attract the wandering attention of children in an era of video games. Companies such as Glock and Clark Custom Guns are helping to fund the United States Practical Shooting Association's (USPSA's) Junior Program.[34]

The USPSA Junior Program Web site also introduces "Camp Shootout," a "practical pistol camp for USPSA Junior Members," for children aged twelve and over. Since 1998, the Junior Camp Shootout has provided USPSA shooters with an opportunity to participate in a summer shooting camp encouraging participants to become adept shooters by practicing on humanoid targets. Children can learn from experienced national and international instructors. The Web site concludes, "By receiving this training early in their shooting careers, participants ...

will shorten the learning curve and avoid many of the mistakes made by other novice shooters."[35]

In addition to NSSF, the National 4-H Shooting Sports program focuses on the development of youth as individuals and as responsible and productive citizens. Its program is designed to teach participants marksmanship, "the safe and responsible use of firearms, the principles of hunting and archery ..."[36]

The NSSF and NRA realize that unless more children participate in gun competitions, the gun industry will continue to decline. *Shooting Sport Retailer* concludes that the greatest threat to the firearm business might be a lack of future customers.[37]

Would you like your children to attend Camp Shootout?

Do you believe that what children need are more handguns?

Children and Guns: Sensible Solutions

In contrast to the organizations that provide guidelines to make schools and society safer for children, David Kopel, a pro-gun advocate, suggests a different approach regarding children and guns. First, he cites several statistics and then contends that they are false. For example:

- Firearms are responsible for the deaths of 45,000 infants, children, and adolescents per year. (American Academy of Pediatrics)

- 135,000 children carry guns to school each day. (Senators Biden and Chaffee)

- Guns are the leading cause of death among older teenagers—white and black—in America. (Newsweek)[38]

Unfortunately, although Kopel frequently quotes U.S. Senators and leading gun control advocates and pro-gun sources, he fails to provide complete citations and context. In addition, he further contends that national statistics suggest that most guns carried by teenagers are for legitimate protection, but does not provide complete citations in support of his argument. He cites a teenager's statement:

> To put it bluntly, I think students bring weapons to school to save their own lives. They have a constant fear of being attacked, whether for money, for drugs, or for some other reason. They feel they need to bring a weapon with them to school.[39]

He claims that, in 1986, there were 41,500 aggravated assaults in schools and 44,000 robberies, but he provides no documentation to support these assertions.

He opposes gun-free school zones, claiming that gun-control advocates suffer from myopia: "The premise is that schools can become safe merely by the legitimate declaration that they are gun-free zones. Until legislatures and the rest of the community begin addressing the root cause of why students (and many teachers) feel a need to carry a firearm for protection, the schools will remain as violent as ever."[40]

He opposes metal detectors in schools, suggesting that they are instruments of social conditioning that pose a serious threat to the Fourth Amendment right to freedom from searches without probable cause. He also believes that decisions about trigger locks and similar devices are best made by each family and opposes banning handguns.

A couple of Kopel's ideas seem appropriate. One idea is to ensure that responsible adults are assigned to monitor playgrounds. Another idea is to establish volunteer student patrols. He also suggests implementing effective juvenile justice solutions such as better juvenile courts, open court records, restitution, increased certainty of punishment, and educating children to have responsible attitudes toward firearms. Kopel continually advocates that children be taught a responsible attitude toward firearms and be taught that America's television and movie industries teach a false image of firearms use, and suggests eliminating some dropout laws and let poor people choose their own schools.[41]

Conclusions

In this chapter, I have discussed the philosophies of the American Academy of Child and Adolescent Psychiatry (AACAP), National Association of School Psychologists (NASP), American Academy of Pediatrics (AAP), Safer Child, Inc. (SCI), and Women against Gun Violence (WAGV). These organizations support decreasing gun availability and increasing gun safety. They promote a nonviolent approach to guns and children and are dedicated to the health and well-being of children of all ages.

In contrast, the views presented in the Jeremiah Project (JP), the NRA's Determination, and Children and Guns: Sensible Solutions sections suggest that social factors are responsible for much of gun violence, that children need to be held responsible for their own behavior, and that *children need more guns.*

Overall, discussing children and guns has made for a difficult journey because, as trite as it sounds, children are our future. Therefore, as a society, we need to continually focus on the relationship between guns and children. As Helen Thomas has written, "Federal statistics show that ten to thirteen children are killed every day by guns in the United States. How long can our society tolerate this tragic number? How many more shootings does the country need to hear the wake-up call?"[42] As children move into adulthood, they will take what they have learned about guns with them. Parents, educators, counselors, and the organizations cited in this chapter need to work together to make the United States a safer place for children. Otherwise, the NRA will continue to win the gun game.

Key Quotation from Chapter 7

Guns are not cool. They are not fun. They are simply a tool—to be handled properly by adults who have a reason to handle them. And whether you believe those adults should be law-abiding citizens—or whether you believe they should include only police and militia—you must make sure that your child knows exactly what to do when confronted with a situation.—SCI

Pro-Gun-Control Organizations for Child Safety

The American Academy of Child and Adolescent Psychiatry
http://www.aacap.org/info families/NationalFacts/99ViolFctSh.htm

The National Association of School Psychologists
http://www.nasponline.org/information/pospaper gun.html

The American Academy of Pediatrics
http://www.aap.org/advocacy/childhealthmonth/Guns.htm

Safer Child, Inc.
http://www.saferchild.org/

Women Against Gun Violence
http://www.wagv.org/women.htm

Other Viewpoints on Guns and Children

The Jeremiah Project
http://www.jeremiahproject.com

NRA's Determination

Josh Sugarmann, *Every handgun Is Aimed at You: The Case for Banning Handguns* (New York: The Free Press, 2001)

Children and Guns: Sensible Solutions
http://www.rkba.org/research/kopel/kids-gun.html

Now, please indicate your level of agreement with the following Guns and Children Questionnaire.

GUNS AND CHILDREN QUESTIONNAIRE

Please indicate your level of agreement with the following statements.

1 = strongly disagree, 2 = disagree, 3 = undecided, 4 = agree, and 5 = strongly agree.

1. _____ Guns are the leading cause of death among older teenagers.

2. _____ We cannot gun-proof our children and adolescents.

3. _____ Metal detectors in schools should be eliminated as they violate the Fourth Amendment right to freedom from searches without probable cause.

4. _____ Gun violence is a critical public-health issue.

5. _____ In the home, all firearms should be unloaded and in a securely locked container.

6. _____ Parents, not the government, should decide whether trigger locks and other devices are best for their family.

7. _____ The best way to decrease gun violence in the home is to remove the gun from the home.

8. _____ Effective child safety locks impair the ability to use a gun for self-defense.

9. _____ Responsible adults should be hired to protect children from gun violence on the playground.

10. _____ Juveniles who commit crimes with guns should be tried as adults.

11. _____ Banning handguns would not decrease crimes committed by teenagers.

12. _____ The presence of firearms poses a significant threat to the safety of our communities.

13. _____ Firearms are responsible for the deaths of 45,000 infants, children, and adolescents per year.

14. _____ The Brady law should be discontinued as it does not prevent crimes against children.

15. _____ Buy-back programs, although well intentioned, are a waste of time and money.

16. _____ Teenagers should be allowed to carry guns to school to protect themselves.

17. _____ Children have the right to be free from gun violence in their homes, streets, schools, places of work, and communities.

18. _____ Gun ammunition should be stored in separate, locked locations.

19. _____ Even though the American Academy of Pediatrics calls for outlawing "deadly air guns," they should not be outlawed, as they result in only two deaths per year in the United States.

20. _____ A gun in the home increases the danger to women and children.

Please review your results by going to the Meaning of Test Results section.

8

Handguns

A single consumer product holds our nation hostage: the handgun.[1]

—Josh Sugarmann

Gun registration is not enough. I've always proposed state licensing ... with some federal standards.[2]

—Former Attorney General Janet Reno

A ban on any firearm is a ban for banning all firearms.[3]

—Wayne LaPierre

If it was up to me, no one but law enforcement officers would own handguns.[4]

—Chicago Mayor Richard Daley

Handguns pose a disastrous threat to your freedom. Your freedom to live without fear of being shot on the street or in your home. Your freedom to bring your children to school without concern they will encounter a handgun in school.[5]

—Handgun Free America

After reading these quotations—especially the Handgun-Free America quotation—it becomes obvious that the easy availability of handguns in the United States is a significant problem to the freedom and to the safety of the citizens and non-citizens of the United States. Before reading the chapter, please think about handguns in America and reflect on the following questions:

- Do you believe that the availability of handguns in the United States makes our country safer or more violent?

- Do you think that law-abiding citizens should be permitted to purchase handguns?

- Do you think that law-abiding citizens should be permitted to purchase a handgun every month?

- Do you think that handguns should be registered?

- Do you believe that handgun owners should be licensed?

- Do you own a handgun?

- Do you believe that handguns should be banned?

HANDGUN STATISTICS

"Handguns are the least common type of firearm found in the American home, yet they account for a disproportionate number of deaths among both firearm homicides and suicides."[6]

The *People's Weekly World* reported: "Every year, 24,000 Americans are killed with handguns in homicides, suicides, and accidents ... handguns manufactured for the sole purpose of killing people."[7] In 1990, an estimated 10,000 murders were committed with handguns. A tally of gun deaths from 1978 to 1997 reveals approximately 300,000 gun homicides. Sugarmann concludes that, of the approximately 350,000 gun suicides, about 241,000 were committed with handguns. During the past two decades, suicide rates have increased significantly among all demographic groups. Over the past forty-five years, approximately one million Americans have died as a result of handguns.[8]

A study at Northwestern University concluded that one out of every four handguns is used in a crime in the United States within ten years of its manufacture. It is estimated that there are 67,000,000 handguns in the United States today. This represents about a third of the nation's firearms and approximately 10 percent of all of the handguns in the world. Approximately one out of four American homes contains a handgun. A National Opinion Research Center (NORC) survey concluded that handguns are most popular in the South and West and least popular in New England and Middle Atlantic states.[9]

GENERAL PUBLIC STATISTICS

A majority of the general public supports handgun registration and the licensing of handgun owners, as shown by the following statistics:

- 85 percent of registered voters favor requiring prospective gun owners to obtain a license before buying a handgun.

- 83 percent of registered voters favor requiring gun owners to register their newly purchased handguns.

- 66 percent of NRA supporters favor handgun-owner licensing.

- 65 percent of NRA supporters favor handgun registration.

- 82 percent of NRA supporters favor universal background checks for all handgun purchases.

- 54 percent of gun owners think that current gun-control laws are not strict enough; 29 percent think they are about right, and 12 percent think they are too strict.

- 73 percent of gun owners favor requiring a license before a handgun is purchased.

- 72 percent of gun owners favor requiring gun owners to register their newly purchased weapons.

- 86 percent of gun owners favor criminal-background checks for all handgun purchases.[10]

Congress has introduced legislation on handgun registration and licensing. Specifically, Senator Diane Feinstein (D-CA) and Representative Martin Meehan (D-MA) have proposed legislation for a registration system and a licensing system which would require that handgun buyers undergo background checks and training on the safe use of handguns. They believe that registration and licensing would promote responsibility among handgun owners and help law enforcement to track down guns that are purchased illegally.[11]

Hillary Clinton, when she was the First Lady, agreed with Senator Feinstein. Clinton stated: "I stand in support of common-sense legislation to license everyone who wishes to purchase a gun. I also believe that every new handgun sale or transfer should be registered in the national registry …"[12]

Joshua Horwitz, executive director of the Educational Fund to Stop Gun Violence (a nonprofit charity), commissioned a poll to survey one thousand registered voters. Lake, Snell, Perry and Associates conducted the poll from May 15 to 21, 2001. The results indicated that more than 80 percent of registered voters supported licensing handgun owners and registering handguns, and that more than 90 percent favored criminal-background checks for all handgun purchasers.[13]

The League of Women Voters Web site states its position on handguns: "Protect the health and safety of citizens through limiting the accessibility and regulating ownership of handguns and semiautomatic assault weapons."[14]

THE COALITION TO STOP GUN VIOLENCE (CSGV)

Based on the public interest in the licensing of handgun owners and the registration of handguns, I am including information from the CSGV. The organization's members generated a list of questions and answers about gun licensing and registration. As you read the following, ask yourself whether you agree with the common-sense approach presented.

> **Question**: "What information is needed to obtain a handgun license?"
>
> **Answer**: "Applicants for a license would need to provide a photograph; pass a thorough background check, including a check for violent misdemeanor convictions, domestic violence, and mental illness; demonstrate knowledge of the laws governing the use, possession, storage, and transfer of handguns; and demonstrate an understanding of firearm safety and competence in handling firearms."
>
> *Doesn't this seem reasonable to protect society?*
>
> **Question**: "Why is handgun registration, in addition to owner licensing, so important to public safety?"
>
> **Answer**: "Registration provides a mechanism for stopping the flow of handguns from the legal market (licensed dealers) to the criminal market. Registration prevents illegal transfers by making the registered owner responsible for

what happens to his or her gun, and by making owners periodically take responsibility for their handguns by re-registering them."[15]

Other questions dealt with in the CSGV document include:

Will licensing and registration make it more difficult for law-abiding citizens to obtain handguns?

What are the components of an effective handgun registration system?

How would licensing and registration keep handguns out of the wrong hands?

Who would maintain handgun records?

This document shows clearly why licensing and registration are necessary.

What do you think?

Should handguns be registered?

Should handgun owners be licensed?

HANDGUNS AND SELF-DEFENSE

The issue of handguns and self-defense has been discussed for over seventy years. You will recall from Chapter 3 that on March 2, 1933, Judge Thompson, before sentencing Giuseppe Zangara to eighty years in prison for attempting to assassinate Franklin D. Roosevelt with a handgun in Miami, said: "The people of this country steadfastly permit the manufacture, sale, and possession of such deadly and useless weapons. I say useless for this reason: A pistol in the hands of you good people of this country is about the most useless weapon of self-defense with which to defend yourself."[16]

Other research reported in *The New England Journal of Medicine* concluded that a gun in the home creates a greater risk of homicide, as it "makes it nearly three times more likely that someone in the family will be murdered by another household member."[17] The researcher found no evidence of a protective effect of having guns in the home. These findings support Manchester's beliefs as cited in Chapter 1.

Chris Bird, author of *The Concealed Handgun Manual: How to Choose, Carry and Shoot a Handgun in Self-Defense*, also concluded that a handgun is the least effective firearm for self-defense and the "hardest firearm to shoot accurately."[18]

Gun advertisers describe handguns as magic talismans that ward off evil forces by their very presence. The reality is that, especially if you have children, you are unlikely to be prepared for conflict, as your gun would probably not be accessible on the spur of the moment.[19]

Millions of citizens, of course, believe that handguns play a virtuous role in a civil society. Sugarmann points out, however, that the "virtuous-use" argument has three serious flaws:

> 1. Guns may discourage owners from avoiding troublesome situations.
>
> 2. "Itchy trigger fingers" in self-defense situations can easily lead to fatal mistakes.
>
> 3. The number of defensive gun uses tells us little about how criminals would react against an armed civilian population.[20]

The gun industry, however, continues to encourage the general public to purchase firearms for protection. Sixty-three percent of handgun owners report possessing their guns for protection from crime, whereas long-gun owners purchase rifles and shotguns primarily for hunting and target-shooting.[21]

Shooting Sports Retailer, a gun industry magazine, noted: "When a child is hurt in a firearm accident, it is often the self-defense gun that is found, played with, and ultimately fired by the youngster."[22]

Eighty-four percent of women handgun owners say that they own their weapons for self-defense; yet women rarely ever use them. For example, in 1997, about 1200 women were killed in handgun homicides. Handguns were used to kill women in 36 percent of all homicides against women. In 1998, only 12.5 percent of women victims were killed by strangers, while 57 percent were killed by intimate acquaintances, 23 percent were killed by casual acquaintances, and 7 percent were killed by family members. Women who know self-defense are safer than those who have a gun for self-defense.[23]

Would you like a handgun for self-defense?

BANNING HANDGUNS

Handgun-Free America, a non-profit organization dedicated to the banning of private handgun ownership in the United States, used the following advertising copy in a drive to increase membership:

> Franklin D. Roosevelt called freedom from fear one of the four essential freedoms. It is time to take back your freedom by showing your support for eradicating the handgun epidemic in America—sign up for your free membership with Handgun-Free America today.[24]

The group reports that ninety-four past and present members of the House of Representatives support banning handguns, while seven past and present Senators also support a ban. Among current senators, Edward Kennedy, John Kerry, Diane Feinstein, and Howard Metzenbaum support banning handguns. The following organizations also support such a ban:

> The American Academy of Pediatrics
> The American Jewish Committee
> The American Psychiatric Association
> The American Public Health Association
> The Child Welfare League of America, Inc.
> The League of Women Voters
> The National Association of School Psychologists
> The National Association of Social Work
> The National Council of Jewish Women, Inc.
> The National Association of Negro Women, Inc.
> The United States Student Association [25]

The general public also strongly supports handgun control:

> Sixty-eight percent favor banning cheap handguns known as "Saturday night specials," 72 percent favor banning semiautomatic assault weapons, 78 percent want laws relating to the sale of firearms to be stricter, 80 percent favor handgun registration, and 95 percent favor a seven-day waiting period for handgun purchases.[26]

The National Opinion Research Center also reported that 51 percent of people from the Middle Atlantic region, 46 percent from the New England region, and 40 percent from the East Northern region support a ban on handguns, while only 27 percent from the West North Central region and 29 percent from the Mountain and West South Central regions support a ban. Approximately 60 percent of respondents in New York support a ban on handguns, while only 10 percent of them report having handguns in their homes.[27]

Dr. Katherine Christoffel, a Chicago pediatrician and spokeswoman for the fifty thousand members of the American Academy of Pediatrics, told the American Medical Association: "Guns are a virus that must be eradicated. Get rid of cigarettes, get rid of secondhand smoke, and you get rid of lung disease. It is the same with guns. Get rid of guns, get rid of bullets, and get rid of the deaths." She stressed that handguns are too dangerous for civilian use. "A handgun in the home turns so many situations lethal."[28]

The GunCite Web site doesn't question the accuracy of the 1997 FBI Uniform Crime Report, which revealed that 55 percent of murders in the United States were committed with handguns. The Web site does, however, report the results of the National Institute of Justice survey that concluded that 72 percent of criminals would switch to sawed-off shotguns if handguns become unavailable.[29]

The Web site claims that, if criminals were unable to obtain handguns, they would use shotguns and rifles. It projects that there might be fewer murder *attempts* with a firearm, but more murder *victims*. Gary Kleck concludes: "If one assumes, probably more realistically, that long guns would be twice as deadly as handguns, then the substitution factor would have to drop below 44% in order for a handgun-only ban to save lives."[30] Their solution appears to be that a handgun ban is unnecessary because more people would die if criminals used sawed off shotguns or rifles. The NRA continues to insist erroneously that the handgun ban is an affront to the Second Amendment and represents a hidden agenda on the part of the gun-control movement.

As mentioned earlier in the chapter, there are approximately 67 million handguns in America. There appears to be a strong linkage between the number of handguns and the number of murders. Sugarmann reports that, in 1995, the Canadian handgun death rate was 3.9 per 100,000; in Australia, it was 2.9 per 100,000; and in England and Wales, it was 0.4 per 100,000. In the United States, however, it was 13.7 per 100,000. The primary difference between these nations and the United States is that they do not allow easy access to handguns.[31]

In 1985, Susan Baker, a public health researcher, responded to the motto "Guns don't kill people; people kill people" by indicating that, although a person who is intent on killing will always be able to find a lethal weapon of some kind, gun deaths are most often the result of a spontaneous argument or fight. If a gun were not handy, many of these deaths would be replaced by a non-fatal injury. She concluded: "Thus, a far more appropriate generality would be that people without guns injure people; guns kill people."[32]

Conclusion

This chapter has focused on handguns in our society. I began by citing statistics about the number of citizens killed by handguns and the percentage of voters who support the licensing and registration of handguns. After reading this chapter, you might be interested in more statistical evidence to support the premise that the availability of handguns increases the number of deaths among all demographic groups. To obtain detailed information, please consult Sugarmann's book. An Internet search for "handgun statistics" would prove fruitful.

The Coalition to Stop Gun Violence Q&A Information Sheet spells out the need for gun registration and licensing. It is hard to believe that anyone reading the information provided would object to registration and licensing.

I also discussed handguns for self-defense. Many testimonials have concluded that handguns are *not* a good method of self-defense. Finally, I discussed banning handguns. Again, statistical data indicates that over 36 percent of Americans believe that handguns should be banned.

Key Quotation from Chapter 8

Handguns are the least common type of firearm found in the American home, yet they account for a disproportionate number of deaths among both firearm homicides and suicides.—Josh Sugarmann

Now, please complete the following Handgun Questionnaire.

HANDGUN QUESTIONNAIRE

Please indicate your level of agreement with the following statements.

1 = strongly disagree, 2 = disagree, 3 = undecided, 4 = agree, and 5 = strongly agree.

1. _____ Handguns are the cause of most of the United States' gun-related problems.

2. _____ Banning handguns will greatly reduce the number of people dying each year.

3. _____ All handguns should be equipped with safety devices.

4. _____ All handgun owners should be required to obtain a license before purchasing a handgun.

5. _____ All handgun owners should be fingerprinted as part of the process to purchase a handgun.

6. _____ All handgun owners should be required to pass a training course in order to purchase a handgun.

7. _____ There should be national registration of all handguns.

8. _____ Handguns should be banned from the general public.

9. _____ The NRA is interested in the safety of children.

10. _____ What children need are more guns.

11. _____ Handguns help women to protect themselves from personal harm.

12. _____ Handguns help women to protect themselves from their spouses or partners.

13. _____ The Second Amendment guarantees every law-abiding citizen the right to purchase a handgun.

14. _____ Handgun registration provides a mechanism for stopping the flow of handguns from the legal market to the criminal market.

15. _____ A handgun is the least effective firearm for self-defense.

16. _____ Gun advertisers paint handguns as magic talismans that ward off evil forces by their very presence.

17. _____ The NRA is concerned about the welfare of children.

18. _____ Handguns are a virus that must be eradicated.

19. _____ A ban on handguns is a ban for banning all firearms.

20. _____ A single consumer product—the handgun—holds our nation hostage.

Please review your results by going to the Meaning of Test Results section.

9

Concealed Handguns

The handgun population explosion of the past thirty years has injected lethality via concealability into every corner of society from our homes to our schools, highways, places of worship, and shopping centers.[1]

—Josh Sugarmann

The gun industry should send me a basket of fruit—our gun efforts have created a new market.[2]

—Tanya Metaksa

The NRA forbids its own members from carrying guns into the NRA's national convention, but they want to force the rest of us to let those people carry guns into our schools, restaurants, parks, sports stadiums, streets, and anywhere else they want.[3]

—www.bradycampaign.org

In Chapter 1, I indicated that part of my motivation to write this book was triggered by the editorials that I read in the *Minnesota Daily*, a student newspaper, advocating concealed weapons at the University of Minnesota. I could not believe that lawmakers and pro-gun groups would push for permitting university employees and students to carry concealed weapons at the university. During June and July of 2003, the *Daily* published several letters and opinion pieces on the so-called "conceal and carry weapon" (CCW) laws in Minnesota. For example, John E. Caile, communication director for the Minnesota pro-gun activist group Minnesota Concealed Carry Reform NOW, wrote an opinion piece that was published in the *Daily* on June 16, 2003. It was titled "A Shift in the Gun Debate," and in it Caile labeled those who disagreed with him as "segregationists, vigilantes, and whiners."[4]

I was outraged by his name-calling and his ridiculous advocacy for allowing people to carry concealed weapons at the school. After reading several editorials and articles on CCW laws in the *Daily*, the *Minneapolis Tribune* and the *St. Paul Pioneer Press*, I decided to write a column for the *Daily* expressing my strong convictions in favor of gun control. My editorial was titled "Ban Concealed Weapons at the U."[5] This editorial was to be published in the *Daily*'s Opinion section. I, however, was informed by the editor that the *Daily* wanted to publish it as a "Web exclusive," which meant that it would be available on the Internet. As I mentioned in Chapter 1, within two days of the publication of the editorial, I had received over 200 e-mails, at least 169 of which opposed my viewpoint. All of the women who sent e-mails supported my opinion that concealed weapons should be banned. Some e-mails labeled me a "communist," "Hitler," and "Nimrod," among other things. One correspondent wrote:

> Whether you are talking about confiscation of firearms in general or the concealing and carrying of firearms in particular, you're still WRONG, Nimrod. Read the Constitution. You obviously don't read correctly, nor do you seem to understand the meaning of "shall not be infringed."

In contrast, Lois Tolly, the director of state legislative affairs for the Brady Campaign to Prevent Gun Violence united with the Million Mom March, wrote: "Thank you for your column on concealed handguns and [for] exposing the misinformation behind the gun lobby's push." She also criticized Caile's editorial, stressing that the International Chiefs of Police—the largest police organization in the United States—supported the concealed weapon ban.

Before we continue this chapter, I would ask that you reflect on the following questions:

- Do you think that law-abiding citizens should be permitted to carry concealed weapons at sporting events? In schools? Department stores? Churches?

- Why do you think the NRA is pushing for CCW laws at the state level?

- Do you think that states with CCW laws will have less crime as a result of these laws?

- Do you know anyone who carries a concealed weapon?

- Do *you* carry a concealed weapon?

- If not, would you *like* to carry a concealed weapon?

- Have you discussed concealed weapons with your peers?

GOOD NEWS! BAD NEWS!

The *good news* in that on July 11, 2003, the regents of the University of Minnesota approved a policy that limits the CCWs on campus. "Under policy, students, employees, and visitors are prohibited from carrying weapons on University property or at U functions, such as football games at the Metrodome."[6] Only law-enforcement officers are allowed to carry weapons at these locations. Those opposed to CCWs had won the campus gun game.

The *bad news* is that Minnesota passed its CCW laws in 2003. The NRA has been quite successful in persuading state legislatures to pass these laws. Thus, the gun lobby, at the state level, continues to win the more widespread gun game.[7]

Restrictions from carrying handguns were prevalent throughout the nineteenth century. These included the famous requirement often seen in the Wild West to "check your gun at the door" of a saloon. Frontier towns established strict gun-control measures to deal with rampant violence. Travelers, for example, were required by local ordinances to check their guns before entering Dodge City, as well as other cow towns.[8] As stated in Chapter 3, after the assassination of President James Garfield, the general public cited concealed weapons as a prime contributor to the spread of deadly violence. Journalists wrote about how easy access to cheap guns enabled criminals to kill with ease.[9]

Although similar ordinances were enforced to some degree during the first half of the twentieth century, crime and murder committed with concealable weapons increased. Attorney General Homer Cummings reported to the House Ways and Means Committee in 1933 that 75 percent of firearm murders were committed with concealable weapons.[10] Thomas Kimball, executive director of National Wildlife Association, stressed the need to keep concealable weapons from criminals, the mentally ill, and juveniles when he addressed the Senate Subcommittee to Investigate Juveniles Delinquency in 1965.[11]

Prior to the mid-1980s, CCW laws were severely limited or nonexistent in most states. In 1986, only eight states had CCW laws. Since the NRA had lost several *federal* gun games in the 1980s and early 1990s, including those involving the Brady Bill and the assault-weapon ban, the organization appears to have made the liberalization of CCW laws at the *state* level its top political priority. By 1998, thirty-one states had passed CCW laws. Today, forty-eight states have them.

Only Wisconsin, Illinois, and the District of Columbia do not have CCW laws. Nine states do not even require applicants to be fingerprinted: Iowa, Kentucky, Maine, Montana, New Hampshire, Pennsylvania, South Dakota, Virginia, and West Virginia.[12]

OPPOSITION TO CCW LAWS

Concealed weapons became criminals' weapon of choice because of their easy concealability and availability. Each state, of course, has compiled data to support or refute the effects of CCW laws. I will use Texas as a sample state. During the 1994 Texas gubernatorial race, candidate George W. Bush and Governor Ann Richards argued about the state's CCW laws. Bush supported them, and Richards opposed them. Bush believed that state residents twenty-one years of age or older without a felony conviction and who had undergone a brief training regimen could carry a concealed weapon. Bush was supported by head NRA lobbyist Tanya Metaksa, who claimed, "People who get [concealed carry] permits ... are law-abiding, upstanding community leaders who merely seek to exercise their right to self-defense."[13]

In contrast, in 1995, Richards said:

> I think the conventional wisdom is that women cannot protect themselves without a gun and I think that impression is fed by males, and the most ludicrous argument I heard during the time I was governor, and also the most consistent argument from males, was: "I don't want the legislation to carry a concealed weapon for myself, I want it for my wife, girlfriend, daughter, 'flesh,' ..." whatever other female you could name. But the reverse was true among the women who came to see me. They said: "For God's sake, do not let these men carry concealed weapons."[14]

Bush won the election and signed CCW laws in Texas in the spring of 1995. After the passage of these laws, the gun industry continued to push legislators to pass CCW laws in other states. The gun industry recognized the importance of selling concealable weapons. In a January 1996 article in *Shooting Industry*, Massad Ayoob claimed that support for concealed carry legislation and the emergence of compact handguns would improve the slump in the firearm market.[15]

Bush, who had predicted that law-abiding citizens who obtained permits to carry concealed weapons would not commit crimes, was proved wrong. During the first three years of the Texas laws (1996–1999), CCW license-holders were arrested almost 2,100 times—they had committed nearly two crimes a day. These crimes included murder, attempted murder, kidnapping, rape/sexual assault, weapons-related offenses, drug offenses, burglary, and theft. [16]

Texas concealed-handgun license-holders were arrested 5,314 times between January 1, 1996 and August 31, 2001. Forty-one of these arrests were for murder and attempted murder. Texas concealed handgun license holders also have been arrested for an average of more than two crimes against children per month, including murder and sexual assault since the laws went into effect.[17]

Karen Brock, a health policy analyst for the Violence Policy Center (VPC), says that the NRA had asserted in 1996 that concealed handgun laws would make Texas a safer place. However:

> The thousands of arrests of concealed handgun license holders demonstrates the exact opposite to be true: license holders are committing crimes, not preventing them. States now considering concealed carry laws should learn from the dire consequences that Texans now live with day-in and day-out.[18]

In contrast to Texas, Missouri citizens voted in 1999 against liberalizing their states CCW laws. This had been the first state referendum on the issue. The NRA had spent almost $4 million (nearly five times the amount the opposition had spent) to win what it called "the last great battle of the 20th century," and lost. Clearly, when asked whether more hidden guns on their streets made them feel safer, a majority of Missouri citizens said no.[19]

ADVOCACY FOR CCW LAWS

John Lott, in *More Guns: Less Crime*, claims that more gun carrying reduces violent crime. His thesis is simple: *more guns equals less crime*. According to Lott, whenever CCW laws are passed, criminals fear confrontation with armed citizens and switch from violent crimes, such as murder, to property crimes, such as car theft.[20]

Among Lott's claims:

- Nondiscretionary concealed-carry permits deter crimes against persons because criminals—fearing for their own lives—don't know which potential victims in a right-to-carry society are armed and which are not.

- States experiencing the greatest reductions in crime are also the ones with the fastest-growing percentages of gun ownership.

- Mass shootings in public places are reduced when law-abiding citizens are allowed to carry concealed handguns.

- Women and racial minorities benefit most from nondiscretionary carry laws.

- Adding minorities and women to police forces increases crime.

- Wealthy criminals deserve preferential legal treatment.[21]

Lott also believes that teachers should be armed: "Allowing teachers and other law-abiding adults to carry concealed handguns in schools would not only make it easier to stop shootings in progress, it could also help deter shootings from ever occurring."[22]

Lott allegedly used the fictitious name "Mary Rosh" to promote his book, *More Guns: Less Crime,* on Amazon.com. Using this alias, he praised and defended himself in online forums and debates with researchers. He was caught when a curious Internet sleuth traced "Mary Rosh" back to Lott's own computer.[23] Using the false identity, he allegedly posted a fake review of his book:

> SAVE YOUR LIFE, READ THIS BOOK—GREAT BUY!!!! If you want to learn about what can stop crime ... this is the book to get. It was very interesting reading and Lott writes very well. He explains things in an understandable commonsense way. I have loaned out my copy a dozen times and while it may have taken some effort to get people started on the book, once they read it no one was disappointed.... If you want a ... book that will explain the facts in a straightforward and clear way, this is the book to get. This is by far the most comprehensive study on crime, let alone on gun control.[24]

Lott claims: "An additional woman carrying a concealed handgun reduces the murder rate for women by about three to four times more than an additional man carrying a concealed handgun reduces the murder rate for men."[25]

Unfortunately for Lott, his research does not pass muster. When other researchers asked to analyze his data, he dubiously claimed that the computer "ate" it. In other words, there is no record of some of the research that he claims was conducted. As a result, Lott was challenged to produce the data or admit that he fabricated the results.

John Donohue, professor of Law at Stanford University and Research Associate at the National Bureau of Economic Research, has conducted a study that examines crime data from across the country. The results, published by the Brookings Institution, demonstrates that the concealed-handgun laws pushed by Lott and the NRA most likely cause *more* crime.[26] Other renowned researchers, including Daniel Webster of the Johns Hopkins Center for Gun Policy and Research, David Hemenway of the Harvard School of Public Health, and Professor Jens Ludwig of Georgetown University, have found numerous errors in the research completed by Lott and his co-author, David Mustard.[27] Brady reported that Mustard himself has admitted that there are gaping flaws in Lott's study:

> ... the study omitted variables which could explain the changes in the crime rates are due to reasons others than changes in CCW laws, and ... the study does not account for major factors that Mustard believes affect crime, including crack cocaine, wealth, drug and alcohol use, and police practices such as community policing.[28]

Gary Kleck, a Florida State University criminologist, also supports the pro-gun side. In his 1991 book *Point Blank*, he concluded from survey data that Americans used guns to defend themselves approximately 1–2 million times per year.[29] Such a huge range sheds doubt upon the validity of Kleck's conclusions. Nevertheless, he found Lott's CCW-law findings implausible. "More likely," he said, "the declines in crime coinciding with relaxation of carry laws were largely attributable to other factors not controlled in the Lott and Mustard analysis."[30]

Capitalism Magazine, a pro-gun source, claims that "A man with a concealed-weapon license who walks along a crowded sidewalk, carrying a pistol in a shoulder holster under his coat, no more poses an objective threat to the lives of pedestrians than a man with a driver's license who drives his car down the same street."[31]

What do you think of this statement?

Which of the men described would you fear more?

The NRA suggests that many more accidental deaths are caused by doctors than by handguns, but the reason we don't ban doctors is that they do more good than harm. The NRA contends that concealed handguns similarly do more good than harm. The NRA, however, does not provide any evidence to support this claim. The gun lobby also believes that the United States is safest when law-abiding citizens have guns with which to ensure their own safety, instead of having to rely on criminals to abide by a no-gun policy.

The NRA also wants to repeal all safety-training requirements and repeal mental-health background-check laws for CCW permits. More tragic than this, the NRA is pushing for new laws that would forbid disclosure of the fact that "Someone who used a gun illegally had a CCW permit—so no one will ever know when people illegally use their CCW-permitted gun to kill or threaten other people."[32]

THE TRUTH ABOUT CONCEALED WEAPONS

Although pro-concealed-weapon groups make many assertions about the need for CCW laws, no reliable and valid statistical evidence supports their viewpoints. In short, legalizing concealed weapons does not make society safer and does not mean less crime. In fact, it makes society less safe and causes more crime to occur. Sarah Brady, chair of the Brady Center to Prevent Gun Violence, stated: "We don't need to make it easier for just anyone to carry a gun nor do we need more concealed handguns on our streets ... The way to fight crime is to punish criminals and to make sure the criminals don't get guns in the first place."[33]

Brady also suggested: "If the gun lobby is truly interested in reducing crime, it should work for common-sense measures like stopping criminals from getting guns at gun shows and limiting handgun sales to one per person per month to cut gun trafficking."[34] Even at the rate of purchasing one handgun per month, a law-abiding citizen could purchase twelve handguns in one year and 120 handguns in ten years.

Why would anyone need to stockpile this many concealable weapons?

Lawmakers also should determine the type of concealable weapon that law-abiding citizens can purchase. For example, they should ban high capacity pistols—called "pocket rockets"—which are designed with no other consideration than killing power in mind.

Why should law-abiding citizens be permitted to purchase "pocket rockets?"

Conclusion

For over two hundred years of the history of our great democracy, legislators knew that CCWs might create a dangerous environment. Several presidents and presidential candidates were killed or wounded by formerly law-abiding citizens carrying concealed weapons. Even in the Wild West, saloon patrons were required to "check their guns at the door." Until 1986, only eight states permitted law-abiding citizens to carry concealed weapons.

Why did the NRA push for state CCW laws? Simply stated, the gun lobby had lost several federal gun games in the 1980s and 1990s, and so it turned to promoting CCW laws at the state level. Since 1986, forty more states have approved CCW laws. These have been gun game victories for the NRA. The gun lobby is also trying to repeal mental-illness background-check laws. Its premise that CCW laws are needed for citizens to exercise their right for self-defense is completely fraudulent. John Lott's research appears to have been fabricated, and he had no alternative but to resort to the old "my computer ate my data" excuse. Perhaps Mary Rosh could help him recover it.

Now that we have discussed the CCW controversy, what is your opinion about concealed weapons laws? Should the United States Congress try to pass CCW laws at the federal level? Should state legislators try to repeal CCW laws?

Key Quotation from Chapter 9

[They said,] "I don't want the legislation to carry a concealed weapon for myself. I want it for my wife, girlfriend, daughter, 'flesh' ... " whatever other female you could name. But the reverse was true among the women who came to see me. They said: "For God's sake, do not let those men carry concealed weapons." –Ann Richards, former Governor of Texas

Now, please complete the following Questionnaire.

CCW-LAW QUESTIONNAIRE

Please indicate your level of agreement with each of the following statements.

1 = strongly disagree, 2 = disagree, 3 = undecided, 4 = agree, and 5 = strongly agree.

1. _____ Our country will be safest when all law-abiding citizens have guns to ensure their own safety.

2. _____ The proliferation of handguns over the past thirty years has injected lethality via concealed weapons into every corner of society.

3. _____ The Constitution guarantees law-abiding citizens the right to carry concealed weapons.

4. _____ I carry a concealed weapon (handgun).

5. _____ Concealed weapons have become criminals' weapons of choice.

6. _____ Citizens who carry concealed weapons do not commit crimes with these weapons.

7. _____ Mass shooting occurrences in public places are reduced when law-abiding citizens are allowed to carry concealed weapons.

8. _____ More concealed guns equals less crime.

9. _____ Teachers should be allowed to carry concealed handguns in schools.

10. _____ Criminals fear confrontation with citizens who carry concealed weapons.

11. _____ A woman carrying a concealed handgun reduces the murder rate for women by three or four times more than a man carrying a concealed handgun reduces the murder rate for men.

12. _____ A law-abiding citizen should be allowed to carry a concealed weapon in church.

13. _____ States experiencing the greatest reduction in crimes are the ones with the fastest-growing percentages of gun ownership.

14. _____ A man with a concealed weapon license who walks along a crowded sidewalk carrying a pistol in a shoulder holster under his coat no more poses an objective threat to the lives of pedestrians than a man with a driver's license who drives his car down the same street.

15. _____ I would like to own a "pocket rocket."

16. _____ The best way to punish criminals is to make sure that they can't purchase concealable weapons in the first place.

17. _____ Concealable weapons should be banned at all sporting events.

18. _____ John Lott's research is credible.

19. _____ All law-abiding citizens should be fingerprinted before being allowed to purchase a concealed weapon.

20. _____ If I had an opportunity to vote for the right to carry a concealed weapon, I would vote "Yes."

Please review your results by going to the Meaning of Test Results section.

10

Reality Time

The licensing process would keep handguns out of the wrong hands in the first place, without affecting the ability of law-abiding citizens to buy firearms.[1]

—The Brady Campaign

Every handgun is aimed at you.[2]

—Josh Sugarmann

Gun licensing and registration would reduce crime.[3]

—Brady Campaign

I am a gun owner. I firmly believe in the Second Amendment right to bear arms. I have rifles, pistols and shotguns, but at the same time I am willing to put up with some level of inconvenience in acquiring guns or having guns in my possession to make sure that I am a responsible citizen who should be allowed to have guns.[4]

—Colin Powell

While you were reading the book I asked you to be an active reader, to take various pencil-and-paper tests and to reflect on many open-ended questions. The guiding question, asked several times in the book, is:

Can we stop the cancer (proliferation of guns) from spreading, or is the gun crisis terminal?

Based on my research, I would now like to change the question into a more open-ended one:

How *do we stop the cancer (proliferation of guns) from spreading?*

I am convinced that gun-control groups can stop the cancer. Now, let's review the highlights of the book.

In Chapter 1, I shared my background with you on the gun issue. When I was a boy, I enjoyed shooting my BB gun and .22, and I also enjoyed hunting small game with a shotgun and deer with a rifle throughout my teenage years. This was a natural part of my environment. The tale of my experiences is, undoubtedly, similar to that of other boys in the 1950s and 1960s. This tale is still true for boys—and, in some cases, girls—living in the Punxsutawney area, as well as in rural areas throughout the United States. I also discussed my experiences in writing my thesis, "The Study of the Rhetorical Events Leading to the Federal Gun Control Act of 1968." My interest in pro-gun-control measures has continued for the past thirty-five years.

In Chapter 2, you read about the Second Amendment and the National Rifle Association. How do you feel about the Second Amendment? Do you believe that it guarantees all law-abiding citizens the "right to bear arms?" Does this right include rifles, shotguns, *and* handguns? Do you believe that all law-abiding citizens have a right to purchase newly designed weapons regardless of the killing power of the weapon? How do you feel about the National Rifle Association? Did you know that the NRA has over four million members? Does it represent your viewpoint concerning the Constitution? Do you agree that law-abiding citizens should be able to purchase as many guns as they want?

Chapter 3 focused on assassinations and attempted assassinations of presidents, a former president, and presidential candidates. Abraham Lincoln, James Garfield, and William McKinley were assassinated with handguns, while a rifle was used to assassinate John F. Kennedy. In addition, assassination attempts were made with handguns on Andrew Jackson, Theodore Roosevelt, Franklin D. Roosevelt, Gerald Ford, and Ronald Reagan. In most cases, the handguns had been *concealed* prior to the assassinations or attempted assassinations. Are you surprised that so little attention had been paid to the registration of handguns prior to the attempted assassination of Franklin D. Roosevelt? Why do you think the NRA is opposed to the licensing and registration of firearms? How do you think the NRA has been able to thwart all attempts to license gun owners and register handguns? Do you think that federal gun-control legislation might have prevented any of the assassination victims' deaths?

Chapters 4 and 5 focused on tracing gun movements from 1922 through 2000 and beyond. Throughout these movements, the NRA continually opposed federal gun-control legislation. Were you surprised that the NRA opposed *all* reasonable legislation? Why has the NRA been so successful at winning gun games?

Chapter 6 focused on guns and women. Again, the NRA continually opposed gun legislation that would have made life safer for women. Had you been aware that so many women's organizations were pushing for more gun-control legislation? Likewise, had you been aware of the many women organizations that *oppose* gun legislation? The preponderance of research definitely establishes that women are at risk. Would banning handguns save women's lives? Would arming women with handguns save women's lives? If there were another Million Mom March, would you take part? Would you be an active participant in pushing for the licensing of gun owners and the registration of all firearms? Would you support banning handguns?

Chapter 7 focused on guns and children. Children in America, because of their access to guns, are more at risk than children in any other industrialized nation. Many organizations continually push for gun legislation to keep guns out of the hands of children. Do you believe that we should arm teenagers? How do you feel about teenagers carrying guns to school? How do you feel about companies that market videogames that focus on gun violence? Do you believe that the NRA is responsible or partially responsible for the gun violence among children? Do you believe that families should determine whether to put safety locks on their firearms? Were you aware that pro-gun organizations are trying to entice children to attend Camp Shootout?

Chapter 8 focused on the handgun. Do you believe that handguns should be treated like cars in that the owners should be licensed and handguns registered? Do you believe that guns are "a virus that should be eradicated?" Do you think that law-abiding citizens should be able to purchase handguns? If so, do you think that law-abiding citizens should be permitted to purchase one handgun a month for an unlimited amount of time?

Chapter 9 focused on concealed weapons. During the nineteenth and early twentieth centuries, many cities and most states banned concealed weapons. Amazingly, only eight states had CCW laws in 1986. The subsequent proliferation of CCW laws occurred at the state level because the NRA and gun lobby groups were losing the gun game at the federal level. Should every law-abiding citizen be permitted to carry a concealed weapon?

Over the course of the first nine chapters, I have tried to present my subjective thoughts on gun-control issues. As I mentioned in Chapter 1, I grew up near Dora, Pennsylvania, a coal-mining and farming community. Hunting is popular in this area, and I enjoyed hunting when I was a boy. I have not addressed hunting at all in this book because I am completely in favor of law-abiding citizens being permitted to own shotguns and rifles for hunting purposes. I don't own any guns now, but, if I still lived in my boyhood community, I would surely own both a shotgun and a rifle.

The purpose of this book is *not* to argue for the confiscation of shotguns and rifles from law-abiding citizens. The president, Congress and public, however, need to address the gun crisis in the United States. *All of the evidence presented in this book makes it clear that the proliferation of guns is a cancer in our society.* This cancer has spread throughout the United States—through the North, West, East and South, in urban and rural areas, in our schools, and among all demographic groups. It continues to spread.

I have studied the Second Amendment for thirty-five years and have concluded that it does not give all law-abiding citizens the untrammeled "right to bear arms." It certainly does *not* guarantee citizens the right to bear any and all arms that the gun industry creates, such as pocket rockets. Even if you believe that the creators of the Constitution believed that all law-abiding citizens—which did not, of course, include women or blacks—had the unrestricted right to bear arms, those lawmakers could not have foreseen either modern technology or the fact that, in the year 2000, there would be over 220 million guns in the United States. Given the number of crimes, murders, rapes, and suicides committed with firearms—especially handguns—it makes a great deal of sense for Congress to revisit the Second Amendment.

The NRA constantly states that the judiciary needs to enforce the laws on the books. For example, Wayne R. LaPierre, executive vice-president of NRA, has stated before the House Judiciary Committee's Subcommittee on Crime that he believes it reasonable to have mandatory background checks for gun-show weapon sales, that it's reasonable to prevent all juveniles convicted of felonies from owning guns for life, that it's reasonable to support the federal Gun-Free Zone Act, and that it's reasonable to expect the full enforcement of federal firearm laws by the federal government. I've asked several liberals if they agree with these statements, and they all do.

Liberals, in contrast, did *not* agree with the following statement:

> We think it's reasonable to demand that when a lawful gun buyer passes the criminal background check and purchases a firearm, records of the transaction be destroyed immediately. What's unreasonable is Lautenberg's decree that we trust government bureaucrats to compile and keep names and addresses and firearm types of millions of honest, legal gun owners for no legitimate law-enforcement purpose.[5]

The NRA position makes no sense at all. If we are interested in the welfare of citizens, records of all guns should be kept from point of manufacture to the point of destruction. The reason we license drivers and register cars is so that we can track drivers and cars throughout their lifetimes. Likewise, we should be able to track guns throughout their lifetimes. One major difference between gun-control advocates and pro-gun groups is that the former group wants to be able to identify the owner of a gun and to track down anyone who is using the gun illegally. *This is just common sense.* As a law-abiding citizen, I would welcome such scrutiny. As Cummings, the attorney general under Roosevelt, stated: "Show me a man who doesn't want his gun registered, and I will show you a man who shouldn't own the gun."[6]

Since the 1920s, legislators and the general public alike have addressed the issue of banning handguns. Over two hundred years ago, the public was outraged when Aaron Burr killed Alexander Hamilton in a duel. Statistics reveal that over 77 percent of murders with firearms are committed with handguns. It is the weapon of choice for criminals. It is also the preferred weapon when citizens commit suicide.

Should handguns be banned? As reported in Chapter 8, approximately one hundred past and present members of the House of Representatives and seven Senators favor banning handguns, and over twenty organizations—including the American Academy of Pediatrics, the American Jewish Society, the Child Welfare League of America, Inc., and the League of Women Voters—support banning handguns.

Eventually, handguns should be banned. State legislators should begin the process by repealing CCW laws. Strong statistical evidence shows that crimes and murders have increased as a result of CCW laws. Legislators should also push for the repeal of the law that allows citizens to purchase a handgun every month. In addition, when federal and state agencies look at the gun record of any citizen, they should be presented with a list of guns owned, registration numbers, and ballistic identification. The state and federal government also should establish a buyback program to encourage citizens to turn in their handguns. For example, on February 4, 2006, the *Minneapolis Star Tribune* reported that "Project Cease Fire, a two-day gun buyback program sponsored by Hennepin County's African American Men Project, the Minneapolis Police Department, and about thirty community organizations,"[7] netted about seventy guns the first day and over two hundred for the two-day period. If this project were repeated over and over in cities and towns throughout the United States, untold thousands of handguns and assault rifles could be collected.

In Chapter 1, I reported that over two hundred books have been written on the gun issue. Almost all of the ones that I have read have a bias toward one side or the other. Many of them present scholarly accounts of the gun issue for a specific time period. Many provide detailed accounts of specific demographic groups.

None, however, has focused on the "gun game."

None has asked you to be an active reader. None has asked you to take pencil-and-paper tests that serve to help you think about your viewpoints on gun issues. None has asked you to make decisions about your involvement with the issue. In short, none has asked you *to become an active participant in the gun game.*

During the twentieth century, over one and a half million people were killed with guns in the United States. In 2003, over thirty thousand deaths occurred as a result of firearms use. Approximately 70 percent of these firearms were handguns. During the past century, the number of guns in the United States has increased over 1000 percent. If pro-gun-control citizens don't become active members in organizations that promote the gun-control agenda, then there might well be a *billion* guns in the United States by the end of the twenty-first century. Those who support the gun-control agenda need to be even more aggressive in their actions than NRA members. One of the most useful things that they can do is to work for pro-gun-control political candidates for all levels of government—candidates who have the courage to fight the pro-gun agenda. Pro-gun-control organizations need to become more organized and more focused on the dissemination of their ideas through Web sites, newsletters, and magazines. The silent majority must become the *active* majority if we are to win the ultimate gun game in the twenty-first century. If we join together, perhaps the following might come true:

All gun laws will be enforced.

All guns will be registered.

All gun-owners will be licensed.

All guns will have trigger locks.

All gun-owners' fingerprints will be recorded.

All gun-owners' photographs will be recorded.

All citizens will be encouraged to turn in their handguns.

All law-abiding citizens will be encouraged to support banning handguns.

All law-abiding citizens will become active members of gun-control advocacy groups.

All mail-ordering of guns will be discontinued.

All handguns will be banned from the general public.

All women will be safe from gun violence.

All children will be safe from gun violence at school and at home.

ALL LAW-ABIDING CITIZENS WILL JOIN TOGETHER TO WIN THE GUN GAME.

Post-test
Gun Game Questionnaire

Please answer the following questions. Write "yes" in the space if you agree with a statement. Write "no" in the space if you disagree with it.

1. _____ The Second Amendment guarantees all law-abiding citizens the "right to bear arms."

2. _____ The NRA is concerned about the welfare of children.

3. _____ There should be a national registration of all handguns.

4. _____ Gun-makers should be held legally responsible for selling guns to illegal gun dealers.

5. _____ The federal government should require serial numbers on all firearms.

6. _____ When a person purchases a gun, he or she should be photographed.

7. _____ There should be national registration of all firearms.

8. _____ A ban on any firearm is a ban on all firearms.

9. _____ Buyback programs, although well intentioned, are a waste of time and money.

10. _____ Citizens who carry concealed weapons do not commit crimes with those weapons.

11. _____ A law-abiding citizen should be permitted to carry a concealed weapon to church.

12. _____ All handguns should be banned from the general public.

13. _____ More concealed weapons equals less crime.

14. _____ The government should allow ammunition shipments through the U.S. Postal Service.

15. _____ Self-defense with a gun is a God-given right.

16. _____ Our country will be safest when all law-abiding citizens have guns to ensure their own safety.

17. _____ I would like to own a "pocket rocket."

18. _____ All gun owners should be licensed.

19. _____ The federal government should ban the mail-order sale of firearms.

20. _____ Guns don't kill people; people kill people.

Please read the Meaning of Test Results section.

Meaning of Test Results

PRETEST Gun Game Questionnaire

If you answered yes to items 3, 4, 5, 6, 7, 12, 18, and 19 and responded no to items 1, 2, 8, 9, 10, 11, 13, 14, 15, 16, 17, and 20, you have a perfect score for the pro-gun-control side.

If you scored 17 or above, you *strongly support* the pro-gun-control side.

If you scored 14 through 16, you *support* the pro-gun-control side.

If you scored 11 through 13, you *slightly support* the pro-gun-control side.

If you scored 10, you do not support either side.

If you scored 9 or below, you support the anti-gun-control side.

As you begin to read this book, do you think your opinions will change?

Chapter 2: The Second Amendment and the National Rifle Association
SA and NRA Questionnaire

If you "strongly agree" or "agree" with items: 2, 4, 5, 6, 7, and 8 and "strongly disagree" or "disagree" with items 1, 3, 9, and 10, you have a perfect score for the pro-gun-control side.

If you were undecided about five of the items, your attitude cannot be determined by the test.

If you have a score between 8 and 10, you *strongly support* the pro-gun-control side.

If you have a score of 6 or 7, you *support* the pro-gun-control side.

If you have a score of 4 or below, you support the anti-gun-control side.

Chapter 4: Gun Movements from 1922 through 1968
Gun Movement Questionnaire: Part 1

If you "strongly agree" or "agree" with all items except 14 and 20, you have a perfect score for the pro-gun control side.

If you were undecided about ten of the items, your attitude cannot be determined by the test.

If you scored 17 or above, you *strongly support* the pro-gun-control side.

If you scored 14 through 16, you *support* the pro-gun-control side.

If you scored 11 through 13 you *slightly support* the pro-gun-control side.

If you score 9 or below, you support the anti-gun-control side.

Chapter 5: Gun Movements from 1986 to Today
Gun Movement Questionnaire: Part 2

If you "strongly agree" or "agree" with all items except 1 and 4, you have a perfect score for the pro-gun-control side.

If you were undecided about ten of the items, your attitude cannot be determined by the test.

If you scored 17 or above, you *strongly support* the pro-gun-control side.

If you scored 14 through 16, you *support* the pro-gun-control side

If you scored 11 through 13, you *slightly support* the pro-gun-control side.

If you scored 9 or below, you support the anti-gun-control side.

Chapter 6: Guns and Women
Guns and Women Questionnaire

If you "strongly agree" or "agree" with items 5, 6, 10, 11, 12, 14, 16, 17, 19, and 20 and "strongly disagree" or "disagree" with items 1, 2, 3, 4, 7, 8, 9, 13, 15, and 18, you have a perfect score with the pro-gun-control side.

If you were undecided about ten of the items, your attitude cannot be determined by the test.

If you scored 17 or above, you *strongly support* the pro-gun-control side.

If you scored 14 through 16, you *support* the pro-gun-control side.

If you scored 11 through 13, you *slightly support* the pro-gun-control side.

If you scored 9 or below, you support the anti-gun-control side.

Chapter 7: Guns and Children
Guns and Children Questionnaire

If you "strongly agree" or "agree" with the items 1, 2, 4, 5, 7, 9, 10, 12, 17, 18, and 20 and "strongly disagree" or "disagree" with items 3, 6, 8, 11, 13, 14, 15, 16, and 19, you have a perfect score with the pro-gun-control side.

If you were undecided about ten of the items, your attitude cannot be determined by the test.

If you scored 17 or above, you *strongly support* the pro-gun-control side.
If you scored 14 through 16, you *support* the pro-gun-control side.
If you scored 11 through 15, you *slightly support* the pro-gun-control side.
If you scored 9 or below, you support the anti-gun-control side.

Chapter 8: Handguns
Handgun Questionnaire

If you "strongly agree" or "agree" with items 1, 2, 3, 4, 5, 6, 7, 8, 14, 15, 16, 18, and 20 and "strongly disagree" or "disagree" with items 9, 10, 11, 12, 13, 17, and 19, you have a perfect score for the pro-gun control side.
If you were undecided about ten of the items, your attitude cannot be determined by the test.
If you scored 17 or above, you strongly support the pro-gun-control side.
If you scored 14 through 16, you support the pro-gun-control side.
If you scored 11 through 13, you slightly support the pro-gun-control side.
If you scored 9 or below, you support the anti-gun-control side.

Chapter 9: Concealed Handguns
CCW Questionnaire

If you "strongly agree" or "agree" with items 2, 5, 16, 17, and 19 and "strongly disagree" or "disagree" with items 1, 3, 4, 6, 7, 8, 9, 10, 11, 12, 13,14, 15, 18 and 20, you have a perfect score for the pro-gun-control side.
If you were undecided about ten of the items, your attitude cannot be determined by the test.
If you scored 17 or above, you *strongly support* the pro-gun-control side.
If you scored 14 through 16, you *support* the pro-gun-control side.
If you scored 11 through 13 you *slightly support* the gun-control side.
If you scored 9 or below, you support the anti-gun-control side.

Post-Test: Gun Game Questionnaire

If you answered "yes" to items: 3, 4, 5, 6, 7, 12, 18, and 19 and responded "no" to items 1, 2, 8, 9, 10, 11, 13, 14, 15, 16, 17, and 20, you have a perfect score for the pro-gun-control side.
If you scored 17 or above, you *strongly support* the pro-gun-control side.
If you scored 14 through 16, you *support* the pro-gun-control side.
If you scored 11 through 13 you *slightly support* the pro-gun-control side.
If you scored 10, you do not support either side.

If you scored 9 or below, you support the anti-gun-control side.

Now that you have completed both the pre-test and post-test, have you changed you position on the gun issue? Would you join pro-gun control groups to help elect pro-gun-control political candidates? Would you be willing to run for political office with gun control as one of your primary issues? Would you participate in a national Million Mom March to express your concern about the gun issue?

At this stage, *what are you willing to do to help our country win the gun game?*

Notes

Chapter 1

1 In Harold F. Williamson, *Winchester: The Gun that Won the West* (New York, 1952), 3.

2 Earl McDowell, *A Study of the Rhetorical Events Leading to the Gun Control Act of 1968*, MA Thesis, West Virginia University (Spring 1971).

3 George Caylor, "Don't Nullify Second Amendment Rights," *Punxsutawney Spirit*, (May 2000).

4 Carl Bakal, *The Right to Bear Arms* (New York: McGraw-Hill Book Co., 1966), 175.

5 Report of the Committee on the Judiciary United States (Washington, D.C.: U.S. Government Printing Office, 1965), 87.

6 *Newsweek* (August 23, 1999).

7 "Gun Issue," *Punxsutawney Spirit* (June 5, 2000) 3.

8 Federal Bureau of Investigation, *Crime in the United States 2002: Uniform Crime Reports.* (Washington, D.C.: U.S. Department of Justice, 2003).

9 William Manchester, "Let Us Turn in Our Guns," *Ladies Home Journal* 167 (November, 1968): 85.

10 Ibid.

11 Earl McDowell, "Ban Concealed Weapons at the U," *Minnesota Daily-Web Exclusive,* (July 14, 2003): 4.

Chapter 2

1 http://bradycampaign.org/facts/issuebriefs/second.asp

2 MacNeil/Lehrer NewsHour, December 16, 1991.

3 United States Constitution, Amendment II.

4 http://www.guncite.com/gc2ndpur.html

5 Deborah Homsher, *Women & Guns: Politics and the Culture of Firearms in America* (London: M. E. Sharpe, 2002), 208.

6 http://www.gunlawsuits.org/defend/second/articles/mythandmean.asp

7 Ibid.

8 Earl R. Kruschke, *The Right to Keep and Bear Arms: A Continuing American Dilemma* (Springfield: IL: Charles C. Thomas, 1985), 34.

9 William J. Brennan, Jr., "The Constitution of the United States: Contemporary Ratification," *Texas Law Review* (1986): 433, 438.

10 http://www.gunlawsuits.org/defend/second/articles/nramyths.asp

11 http://www.bradycampaign.org/facts/issuebriefs/second.asp

12 Constance Crooker, *Gun Control and Gun Rights* (Westport, CT: Greenwood Press, 2003), 112.

13 http://www.nrahq.org/history.asp

14 Ibid.

15 Ibid.

16 National Rifle Association Website: http://www.nra.org

17 http://www.savetheguns.com/nra_membership.htm

18 Ibid.

19 http://www.saf.org/LawReviews/herz1.html

20 http://nraila.org/ActionCenter/GrassRootsActivism.aspx?ID=3

21 http://www.nrahq.org/history.asp

22 http://en.wikipedia.org/wiki/National_Rifle_Association

23 http://www.bradycampaign.org/facts/issuebriefs/second.asp

24 http://www.gunlawsuit.org/defend/second/articles/mythandmean.asp

25 http://www.jointogether.org/gv/isues/problem/history/nra2/

26 http://www.gunlawsuit.org/defend/second/articles/mythandmean.asp

Chapter 3

1 Jerves Anderson, *Guns in American Life* (New York: Random House, 1984), 10.

2 Alexander DeConde, *Gun Violence in America: The Struggle for Control* (Boston: Northeastern University Press, 2001), 45.

3 Quoted in William Weir, *Written with Lead* (Hamden 1992), 30.

4 Lyman Beecher, "The Remedy of Duelling," *Lyman Beecher and the Reform Society: Four Sermons,* 1804–1828, ed. Edwin S. Gaustad (New York, 1972), iii, 24–25, 37, 40.

5 http://en.wikipedia.org/wiki/andrewjackson

6 DeConde, *Gun Violence in America*, 45.

7 Stewart M. Brooks, *Our Murdered Presidents: The Medical Story* (New York, 1966), 25.

8 http://home.att.net/~rjnorton/Lincoln74.html

9 http://home.nycap.rr.com/useless/garfield/index.html

10 Guiteau's words are quoted from *American Violence*, ed. Richard Hofstadter and Michael Wallace (New York, 1970), 413.

11 DeConde, *Gun Violence in America*, 93.

12 Quoted in James W. Clarke, *American Assassins: The Darker Side of Politics* (Princeton, 1982), 39.

13 David Kopel, "Second Amendment in the Nineteenth Century," *Brigham Young University Law Review* 51 (1998): 1510–1511.

14 DeConde, "*Gun Violence in America*," 102.

15 Ibid., 111.

16 Quoted in Arthur M Schlesinger Jr., *The Crisis of the Old Order*, 1919–1933 (Boston, 1957), 465.

17 Ibid.

18 Bakal, *The Right to Bear Arms*, 167.

19 Ibid., 170.

20 Ibid., 175.

21 http://www.trumanlibrary.org/trivia/assassin.htm

22 DeConde, *Gun Violence in America*, 171.

23 Carl Bakal, "The Traffic in Guns," *Harper's Magazine* 229 (Dec., 1964): 63.

24 "Dead Weapons," (Editorial) *Washington Post* (November 27, 1963): 12.

25 Bakal, "The Traffic in Guns," 163.

26 Ibid.

27 John V. Lindsay, "Speaking Out: Too Many People have Guns," *Saturday Evening Post* 234 (Feb. 1, 1964): 12.

28 Bakal, "Right to Bear Arms," 194.

29 "Rifle Unit Split Over Gun Curb," *New York Times* (December 8, 1964): 1.

30 "The Control of Deadly Weapons," *New York Times* (December 8, 1964): 44.

31 http://www.crimemagazine.com/04/bobbykennedy,0527.htm

32 "President Johnson Implores Congress and the United States Government Not to Settle for 'Halfway' Measure on Gun Control," *New York Times* (June 7, 1968): 1.

33 http://www.crime magazine.com/03/Arthurbrener,0914.htm

34 Arthur Bremer, "An Assassin Diary," *Harper's Magazine Press*, New York (1973).

35 DeConde, *Gun Violence in America*, 174.

36 "New York Police Commissioner John M. Murphy, Quoted in Paul Good, "Blam! Blam! Blam! Not Gun Nuts but Pistol Enthusiasts," *New York Time Magazine* (Sept. 17, 1972): 28.

37 http://enwikipedia.org/wiki/LynetteFromme

38 http://enwikipedia.org/wiki/SaraJaneMoore

39 DeConde, *Gun Violence in America*, 215.

40 Wayne LaPierre, *Guns, Crime, and Freedom* (Washington, D. C.: Regnery Publishing, Inc., 1994), 40.

41 Ibid.

42 April 22 and June 16, 1981, *Papers of the President: Ronald Reagan*, 1981 (Washington, D. C., 1982), 373, 522.

43 DeConde, *Gun Violence in America*, 250.

44 http://www.zpub.com/un/be-teer.html

45 Bakal. *The Right to Bear Arms*, 165.

Chapter 4

1 Violence Policy Center

2 Thomas J. Morgan, "United States is the Most Violent Society," *Providence Journal-Bulletin* (November 8, 1995): 5.

3 "Protection from Crime and Violence," *New York Times* (Dec. 3, 1923): 12.

4 Ibid.

5 "Administering Criminal Law Better," *New York Times* (Sept. 8, 1925): 20.

6 "Plan Legislation for Ban of Pistols," New York Times (Sept. 10, 1925): 12.

7 David B. Kopel, *The Samurai, the Mountie, and the Cowboy* (Buffalo, New York, 1992): 74.

8 Bakal, *Right to Bear Arms*, 165.

9 Ibid., 169.

10 Ibid., 170.

11 http://www.bradycampaign.org/legislation/federal/pages.php?page=6fedlaws

12 Bakal, *Right to Bear Arms*, 176.

13 Ibid., 177.

14 http://www.bradycampaign.org/legislation/federal/pages.php?page+6fedlaws

15 Bakal, *Right to Bear Arms*, 180.

16 Ibid.

17 Ibid., 181.

18 Ibid.

19 Ibid., 185.

20 Ibid.

21 Ibid.

22 Ibid., 186.

23 Ibid.

24 Ibid. 187.

25 News Conf., Aug. 20, 1958, *Public Papers of the President of the United States: Dwight D. Eisenhower*, 1958 (Washington, D. C., 1959): 625–26.

26 *Report on Committee on the Judiciary United States* (Washington, D. C.: U.S. Government Printing Office, 1965): 6–7.

27 Ibid., 3.

28 Ibid.

29 Ibid., 4.

30 Ibid., 35.

31 Ibid.

32 Ibid., 90.

33 Ibid., 425.

34 Ibid., 196.

35 Ibid., 256.

36 Ibid., 519.

37 Ibid., 525.

38 Ibid., 325.

39 "Johnson Urges Gun Curb to Prevent New Tragedy," *New York Times* (August 3, 1966): 1.

40 Ibid.

41 "Congress and the National Crime Problem," *Congressional Records* 46 (August September 1967): 221.

42 "The Civil Disobedience Act of 1968," Congressional Digest 47 (April 1968): 98.

43 "Crime Message," *Congressional Digest* 47 (April 1968):103.

44 "Gimbel's," *New York Times* (July 4, 1968): 27.

45 "Store Halts Gun Sale," *New York Times* (June 16, 1968): 1.

46 "Baptist Assails Traffic in Guns," *New York Times* (June 8, 1968): 58.

47 "Queens Residents Granted Amnesty," *New York Times* (July 7, 1968): 52.

48 "Sears to Drop Ads," *New York Times* (June 22, 1968): 67.

49 "Papers Will Curb Gun Ads," *New York Times* (June 27, 1968): 41.

50 "Children Protest Toy Games," *New York Times* (July 28, 1968): 1.

51 "Gun Control a Demand for More Protection for the Innocent," *New York Times* (July 21, 1968): 3.

52 "Rifle Groups Heads Disputes Need for Gun Control," *New York Times* (June 8, 1968): 16.

53 "Overkill: Judiciary Committee Votes to Postpone Future Action," *U. S. News and World Report* 72 (July 8, 1968): 18.

54 "Gun Control Act of 1968," U.S. *Senate Committee of Judiciary* (Sept. 5, 1968): 90.

55 "Schlesinger Says Senator Fought New Gun Club," *New York Times* (June 10, 1968): 29.

56 "Post Office to Give Police Names of Those Getting Guns," *New York Times* (June 13, 1968): 22.

57 "Senate Chief Calls for Caution on Johnson Gun Control Measure," *New York Times* (June 21 1968): 3.

58 http://www.bradycampaign.org/legislation/federal/pages.php?page+6fedlaws

59 "Gun Control Act of 1968," U. S. Senate Committee of Judiciary, 22.

60 DeConde, *Gun Violence in America,* 187.

61 "Gun Control Act of 1968," 58.

Chapter 5

1 "Now Will They Listen?" *America* 118 (June 15, 1968): 763.

2 Bumper Sticker, Maryland, 1990.

3 Joseph Tataro, *Revolt in Cincinnati* (Buffalo: Hawkeye Publishing, 1981), 5–22.

4 Ibid.

5 Gregg L. Carter, *The Gun Control Movement* (New York: Twayne Publishers, 1997), 78.

6 As an "oldtime NRA moderate" wrote in a letter to another NRA moderate, Robert Sherrill: see his *Saturday Evening Post Night Special*, 185–186.

7 LaPierre, "Standing Guard," 7.

8 Osha Davidson, *Under Fire: The NRA and the Battle for Gun Control Rev. ed. (New York*, 1998), 35.

9 Constance E. Crooker, *Gun Control and Gun Rights* (Westport, CT.: Greenwood Press, 2003), 106.

10 Gregg Carter, *The Gun Control Movement*, 83.

11 DeConde, *Gun Violence in America*, 229.

12 Robert Long, ed. *Gun Control*, (New York, 1989), 145–146.

13 Linda Greenhouse, *New York Times* (April 11, 1986): 19.

14 Richard Corrigan, "NRA, Ads, and Money: Hit Police Line in Lobbying Drive," *National Journal* (Jan 4, 1986): 14.

15 http://www.bradycenter.org/about/

16 Deconde. *Gun Violence in America*, 236.

17 Feb. 10 and 17, 1993, Papers of Presidents: William Jefferson Clinton, 1993, I: 76, 117.

19 http://members.aol.com/FalconnnBrady.html

18 Leslie MacAneny, "Americans Tell Congress: Pass Brady Bill, Other Tough Gun Laws," *Gallop Poll Monthly* 330 (March, 1993): 2.

20 http://www.saf.org/LawReviews/Aborn1.html

21 Wayne LaPierre, *Gun, Crime and Freedom*, 93–94.

22 http://members.aol.com/Falconnn/Brady.html

22 Ibid.

23 http://www.bradycampaign.org/facts/research/?page=bradyprev@menu=gvr

24 Ibid.

25 http://www.bradycampaign.org/factsheet/?page=firefacts

26 http://www.cdc.gov/ncipc/wisquars/default.htm

27 NBC's Tom Brokaw, *Discussion on Gun Control with the President* [Clinton].

28 Sarah Brady Chairwoman of Handgun Control, Inc., *U.S. Newswire* (October 18, 1999).

29 Crooker, *Gun Control and Gun Rights*, 96.

30 http://www.saf.org/LawReviews/DeMay1.html

31 Davidson, *Under Fire*, 200.

32 Ibid., 211.

33 Crooker, *Gun Control and Gun Rights*, 96.

34 Ibid.

35 http://www.ncjrs.org/txtfiles/billfs.txt

36 http://www.bradycampaign.org/legislation/federal/pages.php?page+6fedlaws

37 Ibid.

38 http://www.justfacts.com/gun_control.htm

39 U.S. Senate Hearing in 1993.

40 *Washington Times* (December 12, 1993).

41 Carter, *Gun Control Movement*, 85

42 Stephen Teret, Daniel Webster, and Jon Vernick, "Support for New Policies to Regulate Firearms: Results of Two National Surveys," *New England Journal of Medicine* 339(12): 813–818.

43 Carter, *Gun Control Movement*, 86.

44 Neal Knox, "Republicans Promise to Support NRA," *Guns and Ammo* (May 1995): 16.

45 Tanya Metaksa, "United We Stand, Divided We ..." July, 1998, http://www.nra.org.

46 Carter, *The Gun Control Movement*, 88.

47 "House Republicans Send Gun Control Bill to the Floor," *The Gun Owners* 14 (August 15, 1995), 5.

48 DeConde, *Gun Violence in America*, 267–268.

49 Mark Green, "Voting Blocs, Building Blocs," *Nation* (December 9, 1996): 23.

50 http://www.feminist.org/research/report/93_five.html

51 Ibid.

52 Ibid.

53 http://www.bradycampaign.org/facts/factsheets/?page=firefacts

54 http://www.bradycampaign.org/legislation/federal/pages.php?page=6fedlaws

55 http://www.news batch.com/guncontrol.htm

Chapter 6

1 William Manchester, "Let Us Turn in Our Guns," *Ladies Home Journal* 167 (November 1968): 85.

2 Earl McDowell, "Ban Concealed Weapons at the U," Web Exclusive, *Minnesota Daily*, (July 14, 2003).

3 http://www.handgunfree.org/HFAMain/topics/women/default.htm

4 James E. Bailey, "Risk Factors for Violent Death of Women in Home in the Home," *Archives of Internal Medicine*, 157 (1997): 777–782.

5 http://www.handgunfree.org/HFAMain/topic?women/default.htm

6 Ibid.

7 Http://www.bradycampaign.org/facts/factsheets/?page=domviolence

8 Ibid.

9 http://www.handgunfree.org/HFAMain/topics/women/default.htm

10 http://www.iwf.org/initiatives/init_detail.asp?ArticlesID=94

11 Matthew Miller, et. al., "Firearms Availability and Suicide, Homicide, And Unintentional Firearm Deaths among Women," *Journal of Urban Health* 79 (2002): 26–38.

12 *Violence Policy Center, A Deadly Myth: Women, Handguns and Self-Defense,* (Washington, D. C. 2001), 1–2.

13 "The Structure of Family Violence: An Analysis of Selected Incidents," *FBI: Uniform Crime Report* (Washington, D. C., 1998).

14 Susan Glick, "Female Persuasion: How the Firearms Industry Markets to Women and the Reality of Women and Guns," *Violence Policy Center* (Washington, D. C., 1994): 3.

15 http://www.bradycampaign.org/

16 http://www.childrendefense.org/about.aspx

17 http://www.millionmommarch.org/

18 http://search.csmonitor.com/durable/2000/03/27/text/p1s3.html

19 Homsher, *Women and Guns: Politics and the Culture of Firearms in America,* 205.

20 DeConde, *Gun Violence in America,* 294.

21 http://www.millionmommarch.org/

22 Ibid.

23 http://www.matvinc.org/issues/

24 Ibid.

25 http://www.mavia.org/about.html

26 Ibid.

27 http://www.ci.tukwila.wa.us/general/vmavia.htm

28 http://www.armedfemalesofAmerica.com/

29 Ibid.

30 Ibid.

31 http://www.mothersarms.org/

32 http://www.nrahq.org/women

33 http://www.2sisters.org/

34 http://www.wagc.com/

35 Ibid.

Chapter 7

1 Centers for Disease Control, 1997.

2 http://www.jeremiahproject.com/prophecy/nomorals.html

3 http://www.jcfcc.vcn.com/kidsguns.html

4 http://www.childrendefense.org/ss_gvfs_protchild.php

5 FBI Crime Uniform Report, 1999 Table 2.11,18.5.

6 Hallam Hunt, MD, Elsa Malmud, PhD, Nancy L. Brodsky, PhD, and Joan Giannetta, BA, "Exposure to Violence: Psychological and Academic Correlates in Child Witnesses," *Archives of Pediatrics and Adolescent Medicine* 55(December 2001): 1351–1356.

7 Christoffel, Katherine Kaufer, "Handguns and Environments of Children," *Children's Environments* 12 (1995): 42.

8 http://www.childrendefense.org/gunfacts.htm

9 http://www.childrendefense.org?ss_gvfs_prtchild.php

10 http://www.abanet.org/gunviol/youth.html

11 http://www.cnncom/Us/9901/02/rate/index.html

12 Peter Hart Research Associates Poll, July 1999.

13 http://www.infoplease.com/ipa/A0777958.html

14 http://www.ojjdp.ncjrs.org/pubs/reform/chl_C.html

15 http://www.aacap.org/publications/factsfam/firearms.htm

16 http://www.nasponline.org/information/pospaper_gun.html

17 http://www.aap

18 http://www.saferchild.org/

19 http://www.saferchild.org/guns&.htm

20http://www.charityfinders.com/cf/servlet/SIGenerateSite?action=aboutUs.jsp@charity_id

21 http://www.wagv.org/women.htm

22 http://www.waga.org/kidsafe.htm

23 http://www.bradycampaign.org/facts/issuebriefs/cap.asp

24 National Vital Statistics Report, Vol. 49, No. 8, Sept. 21, 2001.

25 Ibid.

26 http://www.bradycampaign.org/facts/issuebriefs/cap.asp

27 http://www.jeremiahproject.com/prophecy/nomorals.html

28 Sugarmann, *Every Handgun Is Aimed at You*: The Case for Banning Handguns (New York: The Free Press, 2001), 117.

29 "Standing Guard," *American Guardian* (March 2000): 6.

30 "Joe Camel with Feathers: How the NRA with the Gun and Tobacco Industry Dollars Use Its Eddie Eagle Program to Market Guns to Kids" (Washington, D. C. Violence Policy Center): 9.

31 Laurie Goodstein, "Teen-Age Poll Finds a Turn to the Traditional," *New York Times* (April 30, 1998): A20.

32 http://www.nssf.org

33 "When your Youngster Wants a Gun …" Pamphlet, *National Shooting Sports Foundation* (1994).

34 Sugarmann, *Every Handgun Is Aimed at You*, 121.

35 http://www.uspsa-juniors.org/camp/camp shootout index.html

36 http://www.4-hshootingsports.org/

37 *Shooting Sports Retailer*, September/October 1998.

38 http://www.rkba.org/research/kopel/kids-gun.html

39 Ibid.

40 Ibid.

41 Ibid.

42 Helen Thomas, "The Supreme Court Should Rule on the Second Amendment," *Punxsutawney Spirit* (March 7, 2001): 4.

Chapter 8

1 Sugarmann, *Every Handgun Is Aimed at You, ix.*

2 Janet Reno, *Boston Globe* (March 21, 2000), A4.

3 LaPierre, Guns, Crime, and Freedom, 91.

4 http://www.freerepublic.com/focus/f-news/912305/posts

5 http://www.handgunfree.org/HFAMain/

6 Josh Sugarmann, *Every Handgun Is Aimed at You*, 39.

7 Tim Wheeler, *People's Weekly World,* December 18, 1993.

8 National Center for Health Statistics, Mortality Data Tapes, and CDC Wonder, wonder.cdc.gov; Internet

9 Ibid.

10 http://www.csgv.org/

11 Ibid.

12 "Hillary Clinton Offers Support for Gun Licensing Bill," CNN.com. (June 20, 2000).

13 http://www.csgv.org/issues/elections/polling/poll_pr_lr_601.cfm

14 http://www.lwv.org/where/promoting/guncontrol.html

15 http://www.csgv.org/issues/licensing/lr_faq.cfm

16 Bakal, *The Right to Bear Arms*, 165.

17 Arthur L Kellermann et al., "Gun Ownership As a Risk Factor for Homicide in the Home," *The New England Journal of Medicine 329, No.* 15 (1993): 1090.

18 Chris Bird, The *Concealed Handgun Manual: How to Choose, Carry, and Shoot a Handgun in Self-Defense* (San Antonio: Privateer Publication, 1998), 40.

19 Michael R. Rand, "Handgun Victimization, Firearm Self-Defense, and Firearm Theft: Guns and Crime," *Crime Data Brief* (Washington, D. C.: Bureau of Justice Statistics, U.S. Department of Justice, April, 1994), 1, 2.

20 Sugarmann, *Every Handgun Is Aimed at You*, 61.

21 Philip Cook and Jean Ludwig, *Guns in America: Results of a Comprehensive National Survey on Firearms Ownership and Use* (Washington D. C. Police Foundation, 1996): 37–38.

22 Galen L. Greer, "The Changing Faces of American Shooting Sports Families: Kids and Parents and Other Cultural Heritage," *Shooting Sports Retailer*, (May/ June 1994), 6, 14.

23 Sugarmann, *Every Handgun Is Aimed at You*, 100–102.

24 http://www.handgunfree.org/HFAMail/

25 http://www.handgunfree.org?HFAMain/resources/support.htm

26 Carl T. Bogus, "How Not to Be the NRA," Tikkun, January/February, 1994.

27 National Center for Health Statistics, Mortality Data Tapes, and CDC Wonder.cdc.gov; Internet

28 http://www.thenewamerica.com//tna/1996/vol2;
Marjolijn Bijlefeld, *People for and against Gun Control: A Biographical Reference* (Westport, CT: Greenwood Press, 1999), 61.

29 http://www.guncite.com/gun_control_gchandgun.html

30 Gary Kleck, *Targeting Guns: Firearms and Their Control* (New York: Walter de Kruyter, Inc., 1997).

31 Lois A. Fingerhut et al., "International Comparative Analysis of Inquiry Mortality," *Advance Data* 303 (October 7, 1988): 18.

32 Susan P. Baker, "Without Guns, Do People Kill People?" *American Journal of Public Health* 75 (June 1985): 587–588.

Chapter 9

1 Sugarmann, *Every Handgun Is Aimed at You*, 6.

2 Alix M. Freedman, "Tinier, Deadlier, Pocket Pistols Are in Vogue," *The Wall Street Journal* (Sept. 12, 1996): B1.

3 http://www.bradycampaign.org/facts/issuebriefs/ccw.asp

4 John E. Caile, "A Shift in the Gun Debate," *Minnesota Daily* (June 16, 2003, ed).

5 Earl McDowell, "Ban Concealed Weapons at the U," *Minnestoa Daily-Web Exclusive* (July 14, 2003).

6 *University of Minnesota Brief*, Vol. 33, No. 23, July 16, 2003.

7 http://www.gun-nuttery.com/carry.php

8 Robert Dykstra, *The Cattle Towns* (Lincoln: University of Nebraska Press, 1968), 39.

9 Deconde, *Gun Violence in America*, 102.

10 Bakal, *Right to Bear Arms*, 165.

11 Report on Committee on the Judiciary United States (Washington, D. C.: U.S. Government Printing Office, 1965), 256.

12 http://www.bradycampaign.org/factsissues/?page=ccw

13 Tanya Metaksa, NRA Press Conference, Dallas, Texas, April 18, 1996.

14 Deborah Homsher, *Women and Guns: Politics and the Culture of Firearms in America*, 92.

15 Massad Ayoob, "Building a Big Market with Handguns," *Shooting Industry* (January 1996): 16.

16 Susan Glick and Marty Langley, "License to Kill, and Kidnap, and Rape, and Drive Drunk: An Update of Arrests of Texas Concealed Handgun License Holders" (Washington, D.C.: Violence Policy Center), 1.

17 http://www.vpc.org/press/02061tk.htm

18 Ibid.

19 http://www.bradycampaign.org/facts/issuebriefs/ccw.asp

20 John R. Lott, Jr., *More Guns: Less Crime: Understanding Crime and Gun Control Laws* (Chicago: University of Chicago Press, 1998).

21 http://www.bradycampaign.org/facts/issues/?page=lott

22 John R. Lott, Jr., "The Real Reason of the School Shooting," *Wall Street Journal*
27 (March 1998).

23 http://www.bradycampaign.org/facts/issuebriefs/lott.asp

24 Ibid.

25 John R Lott, Jr., *More Guns: Less Crime*, 37.

26 www.brookings.edu/dybdocroot/press/books/chapter1/evaluating

27 http://www.bradycampaign.org/facts/issues/?page=lott

28 Ibid.

29 Gary Kleck, *Point Blank: Gun and Violence in America* (New York: Aldine de Grunter, 1991; Gary Kleck and Mark Gertz, "Armed Resistance to Crime: The Prevalence and Nature of Self-Defense with a Gun," *Journal of Criminal Law and Criminology* 86,1 (fall 1995): 1250–187.

30 http://www.bradycampaign.org/facts/issues/?page=lott

31 http://capmag.com/article.asp?ID=62

32 http://www.bradycampaign.org/facts/issues/?page=ccw

33 "Concealed Truth: Concealed Weapons Laws and Trends in Violent Crime in the United States," Handgun Control Inc.

34 Ibid.

Chapter 10

1 Brady Campaign to Prevent Gun Violence, Licensing and Registration: Questions and Answers.

2 Sugarmann, *Every Handgun Is Aimed at you,* 177.

3 Brady Campaign Organization, June 2002, 50.

4 *Washington Post*, 1995.

5 Testimony of Wayne R. LaPierre, Executive Vice-President, NRA, before the House Judiciary Committee Subcommittee on Crime, U.S. House of Representatives May 27, 1999.

6 Carl Bakal, *The Right to Bear Arms*, 175.

7 Telly Colins, "Gun Buy-back Gets the Heat of the Street," *Minneapolis Star Tribune* (February 4, 2006): B1, B5.

Index

978-0-595-43032-1
0-595-43032-5